Changing

by
James Derounian and Chris Smith

Photographs by
Chris Chapman

TABB HOUSE

First published 1988
Tabb House Ltd, 7 Church Street, Padstow, Cornwall, PL28 8BG

ISBN 0 907018 61 0

Sponsored by Shell U.K. Ltd

Typeset by St George Typesetting, Redruth, Cornwall
Printed and Bound in Great Britain by Hartnolls Ltd, Bodmin,
Cornwall

Contents

A Guide to Places in *Changing Devon*

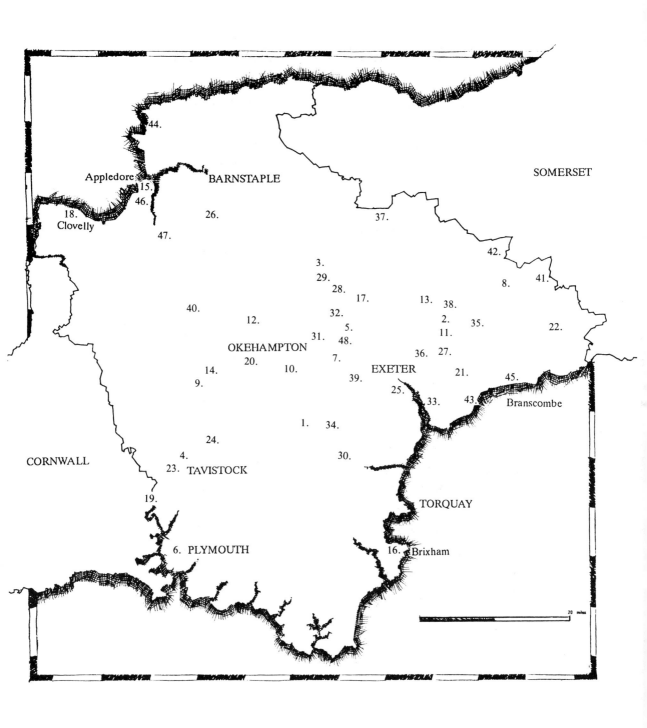

SOMERSET

44.

Appledore   BARNSTAPLE
15.
46.
18.   26.
Clovelly
47.   37.

3.   42.
29.   8.   41.
28.
40.   17.   13. 38.
12.   32.   2. 35.   22.
5.   11.
31. 48.
OKEHAMPTON 7.   36. 27.
20. 10.   EXETER   21.
14.   39.   45.
9.   25.   Branscombe
33.   43.

1. 34.

24.   30.

CORNWALL
4.   TORQUAY
23. TAVISTOCK

19.   16. Brixham
6. PLYMOUTH

20 miles

Acknowledgements

THE authors are grateful to Rodney Vaughan and Shell (UK) Ltd., without whom this project would not have been completed. We also acknowledge the donation of film stock by Ilford Ltd. David Gill designed the illustrative map and thanks to Lesley Linden for nimble fingers on the word processor. The piece on Tavistock's Community Bus is based on Keith Potter's work. Anne Livesey completed the proof-reading.

James Derounian's Changing Devon

D EVON is popularly portrayed as the land of milk and honey; a rural backwater inhabited by bucolic rustics, without a care in the world. Countless television advertisements and media images reinforce this picture of rural tranquillity; the perfect alternative to urban bustle and tension.

But the real countryside has always been a changing, turbulent place; from the displacements of the Enclosure movement to the twentieth-century phenomenon of declining rural communities. Although relatively remote from the corridors of power, Devon has not been immune to these changes: a tiny fraction of the county's workforce now earns its living from the land. The self-sufficient villagers of yesteryear have now been overtaken by the internal combustion engine.

The private car has been the blessing of many otherwise-isolated individuals, but the curse of their communities which have lost shops, post offices, garages and community halls: all because people's mobility has given them the choice – the choice to look outside the vicinity to fulfil their needs.

Five 'Ps' have been coined as essential to village life – the Primary School, Public Transport, Post Office, Parson and Petrol Pump. Publicly provided services have been increasingly beleaguered in recent years. Greater personal mobility, combined with severe constraints on public expenditure, have hastened the passing of local services. But are villages dying? What impact must it make on a community, like Woolfardisworthy in north-west Devon, to have almost half its properties lived in occasionally, as holiday or second homes?

In Devon, as with most of rural England, people are moving back into the countryside . . . but not the same people who used to be there. The new villagers tend to be younger more affluent incomers who do not depend on the community for a livelihood.

Villages have always changed and always will and I believe that the present phase continues a cycle of transition and does not signal their final demise. But villages do not exist in isolation from the rest of society and, as with most areas of life, the ground rules are set by politicians. People complain about the planners, social services, the government – but all these public servants are controlled and directed by elected representatives. The countryside has traditionally been a bastion of Conservatism (with a big and a little c), with this party alignment filtering down from Central Government to the County and District Councils. The age of the independent councils is now well and truly gone.

But what of the parishes – the local people right at ground level:

the third tier of local government? Local Councils are not necessarily the derisory anachronism of popular fiction. Some of them wield considerable financial clout, with budgets running into five figures, which can be used to local advantage. But many of them do not choose to exercise their powers, wrongly thinking that to levy a parish rate is tantamount to frittering away public money. Without local revenue how can these councils do anything for their constituents?

In France the Communes (equivalents of our Parish Councils) employ teachers, decide on planning applications, organise waste disposal and generally act in the local interest. English parishes would perhaps do well to emulate their French counterparts. French politicians also use their local power base as a launch pad for national office; their electorate takes fierce interest in Commune elections because these local bodies choose to exercise considerable power. English parishes will continue to flounder until the electorate takes an active interest in locally contested elections and turns out for public meetings.

Deprivation has become a by-word when discussing rural communities; but the meaning of deprivation has altered over time: lack of basic facilities in individual houses has given way to the loss of basic amenities for the whole community. Ironically the new, more affluent and mobile villagers have brought private wealth at public expense.

Many people no longer need the village store for their weekly shopping; the village hall for their social life; the local school for their children's education. The motor car has broadened rural horizons and impoverished the range of village services. And with the new villager has come a new desire to preserve – to immerse villages in amber as beautiful museum pieces. But too often standing still means slow death. And this is one of the sadnesses of contemporary rural life – the fragility of what is there. Unless people patronise the shop, post office, garage, telephone box, or send their children to the village school, they must fold up through lack of support. Equally, if the face doesn't fit in a village then you may as well wave goodbye to a particular service; if the landlord is particularly cantankerous, for example, then a pub can die on its feet or await new life at the hands of someone who is accepted in that community.

The interesting thing is that community-run initiatives are actually on the increase. In Devon, village halls and playing fields are growing in number. The number of villages with a recreation ground or playing field has shot up from 353 (1982) to 420 (1987) – an increase of sixty-seven. So while publicly provided services continue to wither away, those over which local people have a large measure of control are thriving. This news, particularly in relation to village halls, is not just a good thing in itself; these extra buildings can in turn accommodate new enterprises to fuel regeneration. As our collection shows there are village hall surgeries, post offices, community shops and a host of other multiple uses.

People who come into villages must resist the temptation to freeze them in time – to obstruct new housing and business proposals. Conservation now has wide and popular support, with membership of the National Trust rising above the one million mark and the Royal Society for the Protection of Birds (RSPB) not so very far behind. But conservation does not mean blind preservation. The best of the past must be retained alongside the best of the new.

Professor Gerald Wibberley, an eminent commentator on rural affairs, has described the countryside as being like 'a green jelly' at a party which all the guests want to dip into. This jelly, somehow, has to be apportioned between those who live and work in the countryside, those who visit and look for access and solitude, those who wish to preserve the jelly and those who want to exploit its constituents for profit.

The relationship between farmers and conservationists has traditionally been a tense one; but now the farming and protection lobbies seem to be moving closer and becoming more conciliatory. Perhaps, at last we are moving towards a consensus on how best to manage the green jelly.

CHANGING DEVON is a unique collection of fifty photographs that portrays scenes, events and characters from contemporary rural life. We have tried to remove the rose-tinted spectacles that so often colour our impressions of the countryside and in the following pages you will see images of a vanishing way of country life alongside the new world of industry, computers and declining services – Changing Devon.

Chris Smith's Changing Devon

I'M not a Devonian. As they say in these parts, I'm from 'Up Country'. They also say that it takes about twenty-five years to be accepted as part of the fixtures and fittings, so I've still a way to go, having lived here for some twelve years. My first contact with Devon goes back a long way and illustrates one of the many ways in which this beautiful county is changing.

I grew up in London as part of a large family with two brothers and an older sister. My father ran a chemist shop and for many years took the Smith family on an annual summer pilgrimage to Devon for a week's holiday. My first and abiding memory of Devon revolves around loading the family car, a tank-like grey Morris Oxford, pulling out of the drive and within what could have been only a few miles asking 'How much further is it?'

The actual mileage, of course, couldn't have altered much over time; after all, London and Devon have not moved! But unless my memory is playing tricks we were destined to spend about eight hours spotting car numbers, playing 'I spy' and squabbling in the back of our faithful Morris. In those far off days, the late '50s, our destination was a family-owned guest house at Chagford on the edge of Dartmoor. I can clearly remember Major Hughes and his wife who ran the residence. He always seemed to be away trout fishing! Then there was Mr French, a marvellous old character sporting gaiters, who took us riding; and Eric Hemery was another who deeply impressed me with his boundless wisdom and knowledge of walks across Dartmoor.

The Devon of those days was, I recall, relatively free from tourists, the summers seemed hotter and life generally slower than the pace we were used to in London. I remember my sister endlessly retrieving fishing line, from being snagged on rocks, whilst I tried to catch brown trout at Fingle Bridge; a hardware shop on the square at Chagford which seemed an Aladdin's cave and Rolf Harris! One summer, our last I think, there was a strange bearded man with a funny accent, camping on the guest house lawn. He drew, sang songs accompanied by a string on a broom handle and for us children provided a great thrill because we had seen him on our recently acquired television, with an animal called Olly the Octopus drawn on his hand. Rolf Harris married the hotel owner's daughter; they moved away and our holidays in Devon came to an end.

Twenty years elapsed before I returned. Although childhood memories are perhaps not totally reliable, Devon seemed to me a changed place. A somewhat remote and distant land was obviously now on the map. I was touring with a group called 'The Strawbs' when we came to Paignton. It didn't take hours to reach, as it had done all those years ago, and there were more 'up country accents' than there had been. Devon seemed in touch. My somewhat tortuous route from rock-and-roll to living in Devon took me via a Devon girl, a farmer's daughter. She was a friend of the Strawbs' lead singer. We married in Devon and after a few years returned to live here.

I have been extremely fortunate, through my work for BBC Radio Devon, to have met certainly hundreds of Devon people. It's a great pleasure listening to their stories, learning how things used to be and the ways in which life has changed. Without doubt the arrival of the tractor, modern roads and communications have made an enormous impact on the county. In essence, however, it remains much the same as I remember it from my childhood. At times sleepy and dreamy; at others inspiring in its beauty and, again, exciting – never dull. When I occasionally think of life in the 'big smoke', I realise that I would rather be stuck behind a herd of cows than in a traffic jam or crammed into a tube train. Devon has without doubt changed considerably and when some Devonians mourn the 'good old days', I can both understand and sympathise.

A Small Farm at Manaton

THERE can be few aspects of Devon life which illustrate change quite so sharply as agriculture. Devon is blessed, although sometimes the visitor may decide that 'cursed' would be more appropriate, with sufficient rainfall to make the county good for growing grass. Good grass largely means dairying. Although the milk industry has undergone radical changes over the last few years with the introduction of EEC milk quotas – a limit imposed on each farmer to curb overall milk supply within the European Community – the majority of Devon's farms remain dairy units.

The average size of farm, some 130 acres with a herd of fifty or sixty cows, would probably have been in the same family for several generations. By contrast Pauline James' herd of Guernseys at Manaton, on the edge of Dartmoor, must be unique in Devon. Latchell Farm was started by her father in 1918 when he was invalided out of the Great War. Today it runs to just twenty-six acres, three of which she owns while the rest are rented. Miss James now keeps only

eleven cows, having cut back from fourteen as a result of milk quotas. Each cow has a name – Polly, Bracken, Madge, Broken Tail and so on – whereas in bigger herds the cows are numbered, with ear tags.

The Guernsey is a quiet, gentle breed producing a rich, creamy milk which is sold either from the dairy at Latchell, on the far flung retail round or wholesale to Unigate who collect by the lorry load from her sixty-gallon storage tank. The untreated milk, hand bottled on the farm, comes topped with a distinctive green and gold striped cap to indicate that the milk is from a Channel Island herd.

Pauline uses a contractor to make round-bale silage for winter feed and makes a little hay. She has no tractor and relies on a landrover to do the heavy farm work: a chain from the vehicle goes round a bale of silage so it can be dragged to where it's needed. Even on such a small acreage it's a tough life: "It's just enough to keep me happy, keep the retail milk round supplied and keep the wolf from the door."

Although Pauline James only has a small herd she is keenly aware of agricultural politics. When the government introduced fees for dairy hygiene inspection she took the matter up with her MP who in turn contacted the Minister of Agriculture – but Pauline didn't get a satisfactory reply.

At one time she used to take the landrover onto the moor to cut bracken for winter bedding, a method used for generations before the tractor was even thought of. Not any longer – poor access and cheap straw for the cows have seen to this.

Watching Pauline milking the cows one sees her approach is brisk and business-like but it is equally apparent that she loves what she's doing. The cows seem to understand that and there's a sense of peace about the scene in Flora James' milking parlour. It seems a world away from the contemporary bustle of the high-tech dairy set-up, whilst at the same time providing a glimpse of the way Devon dairy farming used to be.

Payhembury Farm Horses

IN 1987 the special feature at the three-day Devon County Show was 'The Horse'. In a ring, surrounded by static exhibits, there were demonstrations of every aspect of the horse at work and play. The blacksmith and his forge were there, and dressage, side-saddle riding, jumping, a local hunt with its pack of hounds, ponies and Charlie Pinney with his heavy horses.

The horse at work on Devon's farms is still a vivid memory for many people: older farmers and labourers talk fondly of the days of horse-drawn ploughing and harvest time, when the ploughman would walk slowly behind his team and plough an acre a day. How times have changed. Today it's turbo charged, brightly coloured, glossy tractors with reversible ploughs that can tackle acres at a time and plough, harrow and re-seed a piece of ground within hours, not days. The farm horse has not completely disappeared, however, and one man

who still uses them is Charlie Pinney from Payhembury in East Devon.

Charlie is not actually a Devon man. However, he can claim to be from the West Country, coming originally from Dorset, and he does have one of the largest pair of hands in the county, with hands to match and control his heavy Ardennes horses. Charlie Pinney, his wife Lucy and their family, own a farm of just twenty-five acres. Charlie finds a horse easier to start in the morning than a tractor so he has Trojan and Polly as his motive power. These two gentle giants tower above the average human, monuments to the strength and intelligence of the breed and in Charlie's huge hands they respond to a soft word of command or the slightest tug on the long controlling reins.

It's not just a question of being easier to start than a tractor, nor a matter of sentiment that horses provide Charlie with his farm power. Charlie is alert to the needs of good husbandry: "Horses compact the ground less than a tractor and so they do less damage than a heavy tractor and its associated machinery. They are also more controllable and you can get onto the ground earlier in the season – in conditions where a tractor would simply sink."

To watch Charlie, Trojan and Polly at work is to marvel at the understanding Charlie has of his horses and they of him. His knowledge and skill is recognised in places far from his adopted Devon home: a few years ago he was the guest of the French Government at the Paris Agricultural Show, the largest event of its kind in Europe. His interest in horses doesn't just stop with farming; he also runs a business producing modern horse-drawn farm machinery plus implements and he and Lucy have run residential courses on farming with horse-drawn implements.

Charlie's machines have found a market in far away South America and Europe. In Charlie's limited spare time he chairs the Sidmouth Junction Ploughing Match – an annual event at which ploughmen using both tractor and horses test their skills. He is also an active member of the Western Counties Heavy Horse Society which holds an annual event, exclusively for horse teams.

Charlie Pinney at work or in competition is a far cry from contemporary farming which has been overloaded by new technology, where speed is the name of the game and the horse has all but disappeared. Charlie and a few others like him in Devon keep the tradition of horse-drawn farming alive and allow those who are not old enough to remember, to understand a little of what things were like in 'the good old days'.

3

A Blackdog Smallholding

JUST outside the tiny village of Blackdog, near Tiverton in mid
Devon, you find the thirteen-acre smallholding worked by Ted and
Jenny Jury. The average Devon farm is about 130 acres in extent
while Ted and Jenny run a very small enterprise indeed.

At one time they used to buy barley bulls and over ten or eleven
months fatten them on artificial feed stuffs (usually a barley pellet).
Now they keep store cattle, raised conventionally on grass, and
brought inside for the winter to be fed on hay or silage (a fermented
grass feed). The cattle are then sold on to finish before being sent to
slaughter. In their range of outbuildings they also rear dairy heifers for
another farmer to replace young stock in his milking herd. Sometimes
they keep a few pigs.

Jenny is responsible for the calf rearing and also teaches, for half a
day a week at the local primary school. Ted goes out milk recording at

several local farms, taking samples of each cow's milk, determining how much milk she yields and then forwarding this information to the Milk Marketing Board for analysis. Combined with Jenny's teaching income this helps to boosts what might otherwise be a very frugal existence. As Ted says, "We couldn't live on this smallholding if we had a mortgage. It wouldn't be possible."

In Hampshire, they lived next to a farm and had always been interested in agriculture. Fancying themselves as smallholders, they sold their house with a quarter of an acre, and were able to buy the Devon smallholding outright. "It was land prices that made Devon the choice for us. In other words we couldn't do what we wanted at home, so we moved to Devon."

There's a feeling, perhaps reinforced by television images of *The Good Life*, that people who try to make their living from a smallholding are eccentric, or even a bit dotty. "Maybe people do think that we're dotty, because we spend so much time working," says Jenny, "but we enjoy it."

The Jurys have settled for quality of life along with many others in Devon; both are leading lights in the Devon Smallholders' Association. This has seen membership rocket from just a handful to over a hundred. "We've been surprised at how it's taken off and you really can learn an awful lot by getting together and talking."

How did they learn their farming? Had it been a matter of trial and error? Jenny says they were extremely lucky: "The next-door neighbours are farmers and they have given us advice and been of tremendous help, but at the end of the day you do learn from your errors. You've got to be ready to listen and accept that you do make mistakes and then pick yourself up and start again."

To make a start at all is very courageous and given the size of their holding there are those who would consider it foolhardy. But when agriculture is under so much pressure, and farmers with high levels of bank borrowing find it increasingly hard to service their loans, perhaps the Jurys are, after all, at the best end of the farming spectrum. They don't owe vast sums, they don't have enormous overheads and to a large extent they are free to concentrate on, and enjoy, the life that they have chosen.

4

Tenant Farming at Horndon

T HE Mudges are a farming family living at Horndon, near Mary Tavy on the edge of Dartmoor. Horace is a tenant farmer on about fifty-four acres plus four acres of woodland which adjoin the River Tavy. He describes himself as a farmer who does a little bit of everything, somebody who Mrs Thatcher would be proud of. Horace has always lived within his means and only borrowed money very recently, for the first time, to buy a retirement house in Mary Tavy.

"I've always been taught, and I think it's right, never to put all your eggs in one basket. I've got a little bit of several different products. You very often see, when you come to sell, that if one thing is down in price then perhaps another has gone up a bit. One thing counteracts the other. If you have a little bit of each I think you go on all right."

Horace has a small milking herd of fourteen Friesians which he

milks into buckets, transferring the milk into a tank ready for collection by the Milk Marketing Board. He rears his own calves as replacements for the milking herd and also breeds sheep. His father started with the Exmoor breed and Horace followed in his footsteps. They lamb in the middle of March as the weather starts to improve – this is before silage and hay making for the dairy cows. It's not an easy life and his wife, Kathleen, has urged Horace to pack in the milking.

The Dartmoor weather is never far from Horace's mind. "In the summer it can be very nice, but in the winter it can be damned awful." Foxes too present a problem and a threat to new-born lambs. One night Horace and his nephew went out with a flashlight in search of a fox which had killed several lambs. "We went into the field where the ewes and lambs were, and there he was at the top of the field stalking a lamb. He tried to pick the lamb up by the neck, but it was too heavy for him and he was so interested in the lamb that we walked right up to him and shot him. It wasn't no good saying it wasn't he, 'cos us caught him there."

On his sitting room wall Horace proudly displays his cups and rosettes – prizes won for his sheep at Tavistock Fair. It is this pride and fierce determination to succeed against the odds that most impresses about the Mudges. They have three daughters, two of whom have married and live away. When the time finally comes for the Mudges to call it a day, after two generations, the family business will cease to be farming. If Horace has his way that's some time off. For the present they are content with their dogs, cat, sheep and cows. "My parents had a bad time in 1929, but they got through and brought up six of us, so I should think that we'll be able to go on, for a little bit longer anyway."

Crediton Dairy Farming

MICHAEL LEE owns and farms 580 acres at Dowrich near Crediton. It's mainly grassland to support the milking herd, with about fifty acres of woodland and the same acreage of corn, potatoes and maize. 250 black and white Friesians provide Michael with a dual purpose herd. The breed produces good milk and "when she's got to go on, she makes a good beef animal". For Michael the farming year begins in the autumn when his beasts calve. His farm policy has recently changed and instead of rearing the calves, they are now sold at seven to ten days old. This change of direction is dictated entirely by economics and the high market price for young calves. Previously young stock would have been reared on the farm for beef and sold at twelve to eighteen months. The dairy operation is now centre stage.

As autumn changes to winter the cows, as they calve, are kept inside during the night but allowed out by day. In early November the autumn grass has lost its lushness, and with the arrival of winter rains

the ground is usually too wet for the cows even by day. The herd moves into the big shed and yard until spring arrives. As the grass begins to grow again, the herd can be turned out to pasture.

While the cows are overwintered they are divided into three groups – the high yielders or fresh calvers, the medium yielders and the low yielders.

Milking takes place twice a day, at five in the morning and again at three in the afternoon. This is done in what's called a twenty-twenty herringbone parlour. This describes a pit on each side of which ten cows can stand to be milked at any one time. The operator stands below them washing off teats and connecting the milking 'clusters' which are removed automatically when the cow has finished.

There are two men employed to work with the cows, three as tractor drivers and as Michael has just started a pig unit with 150 sows, another man working on this. Michael's three sons also work on the farm – one as chief engineer and another as livestock manager, while the third helps out with the potatoes.

In February and March ''we spread a little dollop of nitrogen on the grass land'' which gets the grass growing and by the end of March with the arrival of better weather the cows begin to yearn for the open fields. ''We usually manage to get them out by the middle of April.'' Not all the grass is grazed and some is set aside to produce the winter feed. About two thirds of the grass is cut in late May for silage, followed by another two or three cuts during the season. ''We've given up hay making as a bad job. It's so dependent on the weather and it seems to me that the harder you work on hay, the worse the quality becomes and for me it's an absolute nightmare.''

Silage is made using Michael's own labour and machinery and also by bringing in a contractor. In this way the silage cutting can be completed in a week. ''It's critical to get the grass cut at the right point so we need help; once we've done that we can cope with the other cuts ourselves.''

Michael's farm is not typical of the average dairy farm in Devon. It's larger, more mechanised and employs more labour but that doesn't mean that Michael is insensitive to his environment. In 1968 he replanted some of the then-derelict woodland and two acres on the farm are preserved as ancient woods of oak and beech. These have been retained in their original state.

Michael Lee is a very vocal branch member of the National Farmers' Union; he attends meetings in London and was a South-West area representative to the Milk Marketing Board. He is keenly aware of both the political and economic pressures on today's farmer. Michael is engaged in traditional dairy farming and he remains acutely aware of the need to adapt if farming, in the accepted sense, is to survive into the 1990s.

6

A Plymouth Farmer

MICHAEL PEARSON is a Devonian who was reared in Plymouth and then studied Economics and Philosophy at the London School of Economics. He became a financial analyst and worked for the Ford Motor Company before returning to Devon, to his father-in-law's farm in the South Hams. His wife, a practising doctor, is one of the Cundy family who own and farm over 2,000 acres. Michael's farm has changed from dairy to arable and beef; now they concentrate on winter cereal crops, oilseed rape, peas and potatoes and they have even experimented with linseed, sunflowers and soya beans whilst maintaining a flock of about 400 ewes and 200 ewe lambs.

Michael can make two unique claims for his farm: first, the grain drying unit is inside Plymouth city boundary, so that part of the land lies within the urban fringe. "This presents all sorts of exciting prospects which we are looking at but not all of them are

agricultural." The other feature is that very little of the total acreage is too steep to plough; this together with the soil type and mild climate make for better cereal growing conditions than elsewhere in Devon.

There's a full time staff of seven including an agronomist – a technical agricultural consultant – and the farm is mechanised to suit production on a grand scale. There are four combines and the corn drill is six metres wide while the sprayer and fertiliser spreader have a reach of an incredible eighteen metres.

These days Michael has little time to get his boots dirty although during the summer it's all hands to the pumps. Managing the 2,800 acres is a full time job in itself, but he makes time for National Farmers' Union business.

He became Chairman of the Devon branch in 1988, having gone to a local meeting in Plympton a few years previously, only to find himself elected to the county cereals committee. "Normally in a branch you spend a long time before becoming Vice-Chairman, then Chairman. You get noted and seen, but with me it didn't quite work out like that." As Devon's Chairman how does he see the future for Devon's farmers, against a backcloth of surpluses and an EEC farm budget under severe pressure?

"Between five and ten per cent of farmers in Devon will be going out of business in the next few years. There's a lot of capital involved and interest rates are high, there's a changing structure and things are very difficult. We're seeing a lot of people in the industry selling both milk and potato quotas; unfortunately they tend to be the smaller units and that's not good for farming and its future. It's on this area that I hope the NFU will focus. We don't want to see people forced out of business because of high borrowing, purchased labour or wrong soil type, but there's no easy panacea. We produce twenty per cent more food than we need within the EEC but we need to co-operate more. Here we grow fifteen acres of potatoes, which would be totally uneconomic in terms of machinery except that I don't have any machinery. I use my neighbour's equipment. That's genuine co-operation and could be the key to the future."

Cider Making at Tedburn St Mary

CIDER has long been a part of Devon life. At one time practically every farm had its own orchard producing apples which were taken into the barn and put in a crusher. The juice was fermented and 'racked off' into barrels and used through the seasons until apple harvest came round again. Cider was part of farm life and at one time even made up some of the farm workers' wages. Payment or provision of a ferkin of cider – a small wooden barrel – was standard and the farmer and his work force would quench their thirst and wash away the dust of the harvest with the amber liquid.

Small domestic orchards have largely disappeared now, although you can still see larger commercial cider orchards in Devon. The latter provide apples for large mechanised production and the farm orchard has become a relic. Some farm cider is still made however, and two exponents of the art are Eric and Peter Bromall, along with Eric's son Ian, on their mixed farm, Lower Uppacott at Tedburn St Mary. The

brothers also have cows, sheep, grow vegetables and potatoes.

The tradition of cider making in the family goes back many years. Eric and Peter's father made cider, as did his father and their mother's father, who was the village blacksmith, also had a cider press in Tedburn. The Bromalls' father used to make cider for sale and delivered it in two sixty-gallon wooden barrels by horse and wagon to Chagford on the edge of Dartmoor one week and to Alphington on the outskirts of Exeter the following week. In their barn, where the cider is produced today, there are photographs of the old cider press. This old press was used until 1975, before modern technology took over. The farm press was a wooden affair and beneath the pressing plate the apples were piled and covered with a layer of straw. A further batch of apples followed and in this way the 'cheese' was built up until the press was lowered, first by hand, and then using the farm horse to screw down the press and extract the juice. The material squeezed out from the sides of the plate was trimmed with a big 'cheese' knife; the press was then opened and the excess added to the pulp. The process was repeated until the pile was crushed dry.

The traditional machine has been replaced by a hydraulic mechanical press. This is more hygienic and efficient perhaps, and a real example of Changing Devon. The straw has given way to nylon cloths interspersed with three inch layers of apples, and instead of pressing downwards the new press moves upwards. The finishing and fermenting process remains much the same with the extracted juice being stored in giant barrels varying in size from 100 gallons to 11,000 gallons. Some of the apples used are grown on the farm and the Bromalls also buy in from other growers.

Depending on the time of year and consequent temperature, the fermenting process takes about three months and the cider is stored in large barrels until it's drawn off into smaller gallon and half gallon containers for sale. Conditions of sale are now strictly controlled and the Bromalls can't just go out selling as their forebears did from the back of a cart. The cider business remains an important part of the farm's income, accounting for about a quarter of its turnover. "It sounds like it's worth doing, but it is not so worthwhile as it used to be. Nowadays the government take too much of it." Strict records have to be kept and the premises are regularly inspected by Customs and Excise Officers. In spite of these restrictions the cider remains pretty much as it was in years gone by. Eric tastes the cider but says he never drinks too much.

"I was put off drinking too much by a man who worked for my father. He used to start drinking cider at ten to seven in the morning and was on it until eleven o'clock at night. That put me off having too much to drink. I like a drink with anybody but I vowed I would never have too much to drink when I was six years old." It's a delicious drink that the Bromalls produce but never underestimate its strength. Devon cider may be the juice of the apple but it's not just apple juice!

8

The Luppitt Inn

AT one time many villages had several cider houses or pubs. They have declined in number with the arrival of radio, television, and the availability of home videos; the pub has slipped from its place of importance in village life.

Once upon a time the pub was the focal point of a village, providing a meeting place, forum for discussion and a centre where farmers could swap views about what the weather was going to do tomorrow. Not any longer.

Today it's difficult to find a pub that's a true local haunt and a meeting place for the community. Many now boast of real ale, beer gardens or children's rooms, others have video games or juke boxes, and pub food has changed from the traditional bread and cheese to scampi in the basket.

It is, however, still possible to find unspoilt Devon pubs and to sample their atmosphere. One such place is the Luppitt Inn in East Devon. Luppitt is a tiny village set above the busy market town of

Honiton. Unless you keep a sharp eye out you could easily miss the village pub because there are no Good Pub Food or Real Ale signs. The Luppitt Inn remains much as it probably was at the turn of the century.

Albie Wright runs the pub with his wife and describes it as a sideline to his farming, although now the farm is largely run by Albie's son.

The inn has just two tiny rooms – a bar stands at the end of one and opens into the kitchen behind. In the summer Albie and his son are busy with their hay making, so the pub simply opens later when they finish farm work. It remains as Albie says ''a place where ordinary people can come for a drink and a game of cards. That's what I keep it for, ordinary people. I know most of them and I enjoy their company.''

He must do, because to have a drink at the Luppitt Inn is rather like being invited into Albie's front room. He's lived in the village all his life and the pub has always been in his house. Albie can remember the American airmen who were based at nearby Dunkeswell during the Second World War. It's now a private airfield but then it was a base for Liberator aircrews and, due to shortages, beer was in short supply. Stocks were supposed to last in those days, but they didn't keep long with the Americans around. ''They were a thirsty lot and certainly livened things up a bit.''

The character of a pub depends on its landlord and Albie Wright's friendly face with his ability to tell a tale and pass the time of day with his customers makes a visit to the Luppitt Inn a real pleasure.

The Highwayman at Sourton

AS you pass The Highwayman pub, driving along the A386 at Sourton, you would be forgiven for thinking that you had come across an escapee from Disneyworld or that you had drunk too much.

Buster and Rita Jones bought the pub in May, 1960. When they and their daughter Sally moved in, the space for their drinking customers measured only nine feet by thirteen, hardly enough space in which to swing Dick Turpin's cat. The rest of the site comprised an old pump house, barn, stable, and kitchen. Making it all sound very easy, Buster and his friends have "converted the buildings and linked them up" as they've gone along.

When Buster came to the pub it was called The New Inn and as it was on the main Plymouth to North Devon highway "My wife thought it would be more romantic to call it The Highwayman, and add a bit of atmosphere".

Buster doesn't know of any legends or stories of highwaymen lying in wait on this stretch of road and describes it as a fantasy, which is as good as any description of his taste in decor. It's totally unlike any other pub. Did Buster have any kind of overall plan or scheme in mind?

"No, not really. I don't plan anything, I just utilise things as I go along. Inside we've tried to create the feel of what an old highwayman's or smugglers' haunt would have been like. It's gone a bit haywire but I think that's why people come to see us."

All the bar counters are made from Dartmoor bog oak and in Rita Jones' Locker Bar the bar is a crushing mill wheel from an old round house.

Children are not allowed inside the pub, but they are not by any means forgotten. "We try to keep them happy outside. If the weather's fine then it's marvellous." It certainly is. It's almost a children's paradise with old Mother Hubbard's shoe concealing an indoor slide and play area, a pumpkin house made from two 1,000 gallon cider vats linked by a bow window and if they get bored with that, an old water wheel in the beer garden that once provided the power for nearby Bridestowe.

It comes as no surprise to learn that people visit the pub from as far away as America, Canada, Australia and India.

"It's unbelievable, really," said Buster. As pubs in Devon go, it certainly is.

The Drewe Arms at Drewsteignton

DREWSTEIGNTON, on the edge of Dartmoor, is a small village perched above one of Devon's best known beauty spots, Fingle Bridge. The pub in the village square boasts a landlady who is almost as well known; Mabel Mudge, aged ninety-two.

'Aunt' Mabel first came to the thatched pub in 1919. Her husband died in 1971 and since then she has run it by herself. Admittedly she does get a lot of help from her staff and regulars. They are allowed to help themselves from the drink room, give Mabel the money and draw up a fireside chair; in The Drewe Arms you won't find a conventional bar! In fact there's very little that is conventional about Mabel's pub. This self-service aspect is the only concession that she

makes to running a modern pub. Here you won't find the juke box or one-armed bandits that so often clutter the bars of Devon pubs. "Oh no," she says, "I'm not going to be worried by any of that. Us sometimes has a little singsong, at weekends as a rule, but you're far better off without that sort of thing."

The pub has changed little since Mabel arrived and it's a listed building so even if she wanted to make changes they would be strictly controlled. But life in Drewsteignton has changed a great deal, she reckons. "You can't compare it today to how it was years ago, can you? I mean to say, all the prices and everything. It's all so expensive you just can't compare. I mean to say that if drink was so dear years ago, as it is today, the men wouldn't be able to have a drink. It's the same with smokes. Mind you, they say we weren't happy years ago, but the men was merry and bright. They come in, have their pint and their little yarns . . ." she chuckles at the memory.

Mabel's energy and recall at ninety-two are remarkable. There are, however, some signs that she's beginning to take things a little easier now. She used to have her own cows which she milked, but she gave up her small holding when her husband died. "When we first came here it was all horses [nowadays there can be an incessant stream of cars up and down the hill to Fingle Bridge] and sometimes there used to be twenty or thirty horses tied up in front of the pub. I can remember the first horse-drawn coach that came out with a party from Exeter to go to the bridge. They got down to the bottom, but there wasn't any room to turn round, so they had to unload all the passengers, who had to walk back up the hill and wait outside the pub until ten at night for the coach to back up. You'd have thought that somebody would have told them wouldn't you?"

It's Mabel's endless catalogue of stories and the obvious enjoyment that she gets from life that make her so popular with countless holiday makers, who base themselves at the pub to explore the beautiful Teign valley. "I've had one couple who have been coming to me for over thirty years." It may sound a long time but it isn't really in comparison to Aunt Mabel's tenure at The Drewe Arms. She's simply become part of the fixtures and fittings, in the nicest possible way of course.

Whiteways of Whimple

AT the heart of lush rolling hills in East Devon is the small village of Whimple. It lies half a mile off the busy A30, which roars and hums with heavy traffic throughout the year. At first sight the village doesn't seem very remarkable, except that it was here that the creators of one of television's first stars, Muffin the Mule, chose to make their home.

Against this rural backcloth, it's surprising to learn that there is a major employer whose family name is known throughout the country – Whiteways. The factory runs alongside the main route through the village and next to the railway line. It employs over 150 people – a considerable workforce – recruited from the village and surrounds. Whiteways, now part of Allied Lyons, trades as Vine Products and Whiteways Ltd., and even runs its own bus service to and from the factory.

At one time the company only produced cider. Although this remains part of the business, cider has taken something of a backseat. Whiteways still own extensive apple orchards around Whimple and from the train they provide a spectacular sight in the early summer when the trees are in full blossom. In the older orchards you don't see the dwarf bush varieties grown by modern cultivation. These are

genetically engineered to assist weed spraying around the base and grass mowing between the rows. However, over the last few years about seventy acres of bush trees have been planted. In the older orchards, throughout the summer months, Whiteways' own sheep graze contentedly in the shade that the trees provide. By autumn, sacks full of ripe apples are stacked against the knarled trunks ready for transport to Showerings at Shepton Mallett (in Somerset). Here they are pressed and the resulting apple juice returned to Whimple, or nearby Hele, for storage and fermentation.

Although cider is still a popular drink, the family business diversified into the production of wines and has recently concentrated on light British Wines. 'Concorde', slightly sparkling, 'Rougemont Castle', a red and white British wine named after the ruins of a castle in Exeter, and 'Sanatogen' are Whiteways' market leaders. Inside the factory the traditional cider press can still be seen by visitors. Now they ferment, bottle and can the products on a modern automated bottling and canning line, for both the export and home markets.

Whiteways typifies the importance of moving with the times. It has recognised the need to diversify, meet market demands and create trends whilst retaining its local roots. Even so, it is still hard to believe that in this quiet East Devon village there's a thriving, modern, drink manufacturer whose products are known and enjoyed worldwide.

North Tawton Cheese Factory

QUAINT thoughts of cheese making as a cottage industry are immediately dispelled on a visit to Express Foods Factory at North Tawton, near Okehampton. 160 people turn the milk, supplied from 700 farms, into Cheddar cheese.

The factory is a bit like the Windmill Theatre, in that it never closes and production continues all day, every day, weekends included. The milk comes farm fresh and is stored in giant silos before being pumped into the dairy for pasturisation. Each stage of manufacture is carefully monitored; both timing and temperature are critical. The raw milk is heated to 161 degrees F, held for fifteen seconds, before being cooled again to 88 degrees when the cheese starter is added. From the pasturising unit it passes into cheese vats.

The liquid is continually stirred by giant paddles for two hours forty minutes, and it is during this stage that you can see the first signs of the cheese settling out and solidifying. To gain some impression of the scale of the operation you have to realise that the factory is handling ten thousand gallons of milk each hour, which equals about four and a half thousand tons of cheese!

Once this process is complete the vats are emptied. The whey or liquid is separated from the solid material which at this point resembles scrambled egg or curds. The whole process is regulated from

a computerised control room that looks like the bridge of a modern warship. The curd is then fed automatically to the 'cheddarmaster' which is the hub of the whole operation.

There are three stages. First the curds are drained off before being blown into the top of a tower, which can hold ten tons at any one time. It stays in the tower for two hours, and during this time the curd cheddars. The cheddared curd looks and feels like chicken breasts, very elastic, because the curds have joined and knitted together. Next, they are milled into half inch squares and salt is added before pressing.

The salted curd is fed to block-forming equipment where it is pressed to form a block 14" x 11" x 7" high. The slabs of cheese are then vacuum packed and wrapped in strong cardboard cartons, before being cooled and passed to the cold store to mature. After several months the cheese is transported to Oswestry in Shropshire for final packaging and distribution.

Nothing is wasted because the whey, or by-product of the cheese making, is put through an evaporation process. The resulting dried powder is used as animal feed or in the food industry for soups and baking.

North Tawton's cheese factory is another example of modern highly technical work taking place in Devon's heartland.

Hele Paper Mill

P APER is part of our daily lives. We write on it, read news printed on it, we buy things wrapped in it, put it on our walls and most things that we do have some connection with paper or paper products.

Different kinds of paper have been made at the Hele Paper Mill (a mile from Bradnich, near Exeter) since the mid 1700s. The mill, in various private ownerships until 1890, was operated for thirty years until 1920 by the Hele Paper Company. In 1920 it was bought by the Wiggins Teape Group who sold it on to J. Bibby and Sons in June 1987. The mill currently provides work for 160 people. Half of these are on a continuous shift system to keep the mill operating from 6 a.m. on Monday until the machinery shuts down at 6 p.m. the following Saturday.

Devon Valley Industries use the following materials: woodpulp,

cottons, a particular variety of grass, manilla and some man-made fibres such as rayon; all are part of the 'furnish' or recipe used to make the different papers. The process is rather like home cooking, although on a massive scale. To the various fibres, different chemicals are added – starch, resins, acids, dyes and so on. All of these ingredients combine with large amounts of water in a giant mixer or pulper. Here they are thoroughly mashed into a wet slushy mixture, similar in texture to *papier maché*.

A lot more water is added and the fibres are further separated by passing through refiners, before being fed onto the paper-making machine. The 'stuff', as it is commonly known, passes along a fine mesh belt known as the wire; much of the water drains away leaving the fibres forming a web of paper. This then passes over steam-heated cylinders to produce papers known as 'Industrial Intermediates'. In layman's terms this means papers suitable for use in oil, air and fuel filters for cars, dust bags for vacuum cleaners, the surface paper for laminates found on kitchen units and other furniture, and as absorbent pads placed at the bottom of pre-packed meats, on supermarket shelves. These papers require a high degree of technology, skill and expertise.

Hele Paper Products travel far beyond the county boundary to Europe, Australia, India, Africa and the Middle East – living proof of Devon business with strong international connections.

Meldon Quarry

MELDON QUARRY is just off the main A30 road beyond Okehampton. Owned by British Rail, it was previously bought in 1897 by the London and South Western Railway to produce ballast, which is quite literally the foundation of the railway; steel rails sit on wooden or concrete sleepers which in turn are bedded on ballast, or giant chippings.

Sited at the edge of Dartmoor, you might expect that granite is quarried at Meldon but in fact it's a rock called hornfels which is excavated and then processed. With the advent of high-speed trains in the 1970s, the limestone ballast then in use was cracking under the strain. Harder rock was called for and hornfels fitted the bill. It's a metamorphic rock formed by heat and pressure acting on the granite as it was pushed through to form the mass of Dartmoor. The rock at

Meldon Quarry railway sidings

Meldon diffused into a solid state to become glassy and it is this quality which makes it ideal for ballast.

Meldon covers 230 acres and employs sixty people in the quarrying. The top soil is removed and used subsequently for landscaping once a section has been quarried. Vertical holes are then drilled into the rock, explosive charges set and the rock blasted. If the explosives have done their job the material is of small enough size to be loaded into dumper trucks. These huge machines weigh thirty to forty tons apiece and transport material to the primary crusher – a terrifying conical grinding machine which rubs and smashes the rock to a smaller size. If the stone is still too big to handle before going into the crusher, it is broken down by giant 'drop ball' machines, which hoist a big metal ball high into the air before dropping it on the rock beneath. The primary crusher can reduce rock which measures about 28 inches by 100 inches to pieces 5 inches by 12 inches. This is then moved via a series of feeders and conveyor belts to the secondary crusher, which further reduces the rock to pieces two inches by three quarters of an inch. This is the size required for ballast. The whole process, from the time the dumpers tip their load into the primary crusher can take as little as five minutes and each day Meldon produces around 2,000 tons.

The ballast is mechanically loaded into waiting railway trucks in the sidings at Meldon and the line subsequently joins the main railway network. Meldon runs twenty-five trains each week to supply what Tony Dumpleton, the quarry manager, calls "quite literally the foundation of the railway".

The process is inherently dangerous but the safety record at Meldon is very good, perhaps due to the evolution of more stable explosives. Over the last ten years accidents have been few. Just after the war two quarry workers were killed when they accidentally drilled into some undetonated explosives but with the advent of newer types of charge, such an accident is impossible today.

There are those who view Meldon as a blot on the landscape, as a desecration of Dartmoor, but it is impressive to see the care with which exhausted benches, or quarry steps, are reinstated, landscaped and planted with trees. These are not just a blanket of conifers but include traditional hard woods such as beech and oak. As with any quarrying it's inevitable that some disturbance of the countryside will occur. At Meldon, with increasing awareness of the environment, it seems that modern technology and the Devon landscape can live in harmony.

15

Appledore Shipyard

AS the sea is part of Devon, it follows that shipbuilding is as well. Appledore-Fergusson, the shipyard at Bideford in North Devon, provides a highlight in what is generally considered an unemployment blackspot. Work, other than seasonal summer employment, is hard to come by, so a firm which has a labour force of 530 is good news. But every silver cloud has a dark lining, to twist a well known phrase. The biggest problem is to keep the orders flowing in so that the workforce is continually occupied.

The shipyard, part of the nationalised British Shipbuilders' Corporation, has found a market niche which has boosted Appledore's trade over the last twenty years. The search for gravel and aggregate has moved from the land to the sea, and with it has arisen the dredger. The dredger, a highly complex and sophisticated vessel, forms a major part of the yard's business. The simple bulk-carrier has

Launch of the dredger Arco Adur

become almost exclusively the province of Far Eastern manufacturers.

Appledore is aware that the home market alone cannot keep the yard afloat. Sales staff are deployed world-wide to secure orders which may take months to clinch because of legal and financial complexities. No one pops out to buy a ship just because it's a fine afternoon! China is one rapidly expanding market.

In the yard's covered dock they can build two or three ships a year of up to 10,000 tons. A boat of three hundred feet in length, as long as a football pitch, can be built and floated from the dock. Ships are not launched in the traditional manner down a slip-way, but instead the dock gates are opened, the tide comes in and the finished ship is floated out to its new owner.

It all sounds straightforward, but for the yard's management the constant headache is one of keeping the order book full. Gone are the days of finishing one ship and starting on the next. Today it's a highly competitive market and the staff recognise that government funding cannot continue forever; in the meantime the public have a right to expect value for money from the yard.

At one time there were over 800 employed at Appledore but now it has slimmed down and to survive the yard must deliver orders to specification and on time. The yard is the pivotal point of the local economy where almost every raw material that you can imagine is assembled – steel, wood, glass and so on. There's little doubt that within Devon and further afield, Appledore shipyard has put its home base of Bideford on the map and that is exactly where they intend it should stay.

Brixham Fishing

DEVON is bounded by the sea to north and south, so it's hardly surprising that the ocean should figure prominently in the county's history. Perhaps the best known local hero is Sir Francis Drake who played bowls on Plymouth Hoe as the Spanish Armada sailed into sight in 1588. Until recently Brixham harbour provided a safe haven for a replica of Drake's ship *The Golden Hind* which, sadly, sank on an off-shore trip during 1987.

The smell of salt air and the incessant screech of seagulls are an integral part of any fish market, and Brixham is still a big fishing centre with a busy market and a cluster of harbour-side fish shops and fishermen's pubs.

The port is home to both beamers and trawlers – a beamer is a boat of about twelve hundred horse power, whereas a trawler is somewhat smaller – sometimes called a dayawler – at about three hundred horse

power. The smaller boats leave harbour and return the same day while the larger beamers will be away for days at a time. The beamers use two nets, whereas a trawler has just one. The beamer is better equipped to catch the prime fish to be found in the seas off Brixham and beyond, such as the Dover sole. The beamer can work day and night using three tons of net, chain and tackle on each side of the boat to dig the prized sole out from the mud of the ocean bed. Turbot and brill are also much sought after and Brixham has a reputation for quality fish.

The beamer has a crew of six, the trawler just three. On the beamers the crew never want for the luxuries of life; the're a television and even video on board. The fishermen work in shifts; the captain and his mate do twelve hours on and twelve off, with the remainder of the crew working six on and six off.

There's no sense of any decline in the industry, and in spite of the rigours of life at sea, more boats than ever seem to fish from Brixham and there are currently about 107 boats of varying sizes which call Brixham their home port. The fish they catch is washed, cleaned and packed in ice boxes on board, ready to come ashore on their return. The catch is then tipped onto tables, sorted and graded ready for auction at the quayside market.

There's an auction every week-day morning and the fish is sold in six stone lots to the highest bidder. It's hard to realise that the fish in the market has come from all round the British Isles, whatever the weather! A hard way to earn a living? George Dyer, who used to fish and now works in the market, reckons it is. "Yeah. But it's got its good points. You work hard and play hard, sort of thing. It's all or nothing, but it's a good life."

It's a life that certainly is important to Brixham. Fishing here is very much a family concern and if it's difficult to forget the sea in Devon, at Brixham it's impossible. There is one cloud on the horizon: a marina is to be built which, many fear, will jeopardise the uniqueness of Brixham as a fishing port.

Building With Cob

THE popular image of Devon includes the picture postcard village of thatched, white cob-walled cottages and indeed much original cob does still exist throughout the county. Alf Howard who lives in Down St Mary, mid Devon, reckons that cob has been used for building since the twelfth century. So what makes it such a durable material?

Cob is subsoil mixed with winter-grown straw. Alf says that you mustn't select too good a clay, otherwise it cracks, and straw from corn drilled in the autumn and harvested the following late summer is ideal: the process of overwintering adds to its strength. Straw binds the subsoil together; traditionally the mixing of these two was done using several bullocks. The shape of this animal's foot is ideal for pushing the straw into the soil. A man's foot may be no good for the job of mixing but is ideal for the laying of cob onto a wall and pressing it down. pushing the straw into the soil. A man's foot may be no good for the job of mixing but is ideal for the laying of cob onto a wall and pressing it down.

The consistency of the mixture is a matter of experience, just like home cooking. Alf used to watch his mother baking, throwing in a handful of this and a handful of that, with a little drop of water, until she had it just right. "It's just the same with cob. You mustn't have it too soft and you mustn't have it too stiff. It's something that you have to learn by using it."

One of the popular misconceptions is that cow dung was added to the mixture, but Alf says that this is altogether wrong. "Years ago when they trod it up with two little bullocks what actually happened was that the bullocks used to leave their card behind before they left work and that's how the dung got into the cob, but it was never added. The only time we added cow dung was when we used to parge (plaster line) the chimneys because the dung would kill the acid in smoke and stop the corrosion in a chimney. We also used cow dung mixed up with a bit of water to kill the smoke stains on the ceiling before we whitewashed it. We called it arse acid because we couldn't tell the farmer's wife we were using cow dung on her ceiling."

After the mix has been made the construction of a cob wall can start. But, Alf says, "Cob is like a baby. It's got to have a dry hat and a dry bottom." The hat is the thatch and the dry bottom is the stone wall which is the foundation onto which the cob is laid. It provides the damp course. Some think that a glass screen was used to hold back the damp in later years but Alf says not. "In more recent years they sometimes used to add broken bits of glass on top of the stone, between it and the cob, to stop the rats burrowing into the walls, but in the early days, of course, they hadn't got glass."

The cob is built up in steps from the base, compressed and compacted. The more it's compressed, the better the wall. But the wall has to breathe, says Alf; "The biggest detriment a cob wall can have is when they plaster it up with cement rendering. It's just like you and me. We've got to breathe; well, so has the cob."

If the image of building in cob is that it's a thing of the past, Alf Howard is living proof that the craft is very much alive. The village of Down St Mary boasts a cob bus shelter that Alf and his friends built and he reckons that traditional building methods using cob and wood are once again becoming popular. Devon may not be changing so much after all.

18

Clovelly

CLOVELLY, on the North Devon coast, is about eleven miles from Bideford and has a world-wide reputation as a place of outstanding natural beauty. The narrow cobbled street – Clovelly's high street is called "Up-a-Long" or "Down-a-Long" depending on which way you are going – drops steeply down between rows of picturesque houses to the walled harbour below.

The harbour explains the very reason for Clovelly's existence: at one time the village supported a thriving fishing industry founded on the abundant herring shoals which flourished off shore. Now the herring have largely disappeared and with it Clovelly's most important industry. Today, without doubt, tourism has replaced fishing and people travel from all over the world to sample the atmosphere of a village which time seems to have passed by. Traffic, aside from essential service vehicles such as the ambulance, is not allowed beyond

the car park at the top of the village and supplies have to be carried down by donkey or hand-drawn sledges. Once the donkeys transported herring and today they provide the tourist with a holiday snapshot, but in essence Clovelly has changed very little through the years. There used to be an open stream which ran alongside the main street, but for health reasons this now runs underground as do all the mains services for Clovelly. The village is thus spared a clutter of telegraph poles, electricity pylons or overhead wires.

There is little doubt that the best time to visit the village is during the autumn or winter months. Summer visitors have disappeared and the village settles down to a relatively undisturbed period, except for the weather which rushes in from the sea with occasional ferocity. It seems that the annual pilgrimage of holidaymakers certainly hasn't changed, at least for the last hundred years or so. Clovelly was first put on the map by Charles Kingsley in his book *Westward Ho*. In the late nineteenth century Kingsley's son-in-law, the Reverend William Harrison, then rector of Clovelly, wrote, 'Those were the prehistoric days of silence and solitude, when the life of the place went on undisturbed and untroubled by the big world around.

'It is very different now – at any rate for six months of the year. There are days when the little village is like a fair; when the visitors arrive in troops and battalions, by sea and land, and with frank simplicity of mind take all possible pains to destroy the sense of beauty and repose and quiet which they are supposed to value and seek.'

Those words could well have been written today. Visitors flock in their thousands to see the winding cobbled street and the famous donkeys but as the summer sun, if we are lucky enough to get any, fades and autumn arrives, peace returns to Clovelly and the lovely village is once more left to those who live and work there, and to the elements . . . at least until next spring.

Morwellham Quay

MUSEUMS can be dry, dusty, dull places, painful reminders of history lessons where text book stories never came to life but remained distant and incomprehensible. By contrast on the River Tamar, a few miles from the ancient Stannary (lead mining) town of Tavistock, is Morwellham which has been lovingly restored by a charitable trust. It illustrates in graphic detail the life of a great inland port, how it worked and why it was there.

In the second half of the nineteenth century, valuable mineral deposits were found in the hills which sweep down to the Tamar at this point. These were mined and output became so great that a secondary industry sprang up to process and transport the minerals.

In 1858 an inland dock was built, capable of taking ships of 300 tons. Before this, ore from Dartmoor mines came to Morwellham by barge on the Tavistock Canal. Having been processed at Morwellham

Quay, the extracted mineral was auctioned to the highest bidder and shipped out of the port. At this stage Morwellham Quay was a thriving, busy port but as the mines became exhausted and the mineral seams ran out, so the shafts closed and Morwellham fell into disuse and decay.

Today however, although the mines are no longer working, Morwellham Quay has undergone extensive restoration. The derelict dock is now once more visible, giving the visitor a good idea of the scale of this industrial operation. The giant water wheel, which dominates the quay and supplied Morwellham with its power, now turns again and its sheer size is breathtaking. Perhaps the most impressive aspect of the restoration is the quay and surrounding buildings which have been brought back to life. They bustle with village characters all dressed in period costume. These characters explain to the visitor their task and function in the working of Morwellham. The carpenter, barrel maker and the man who analyses and weighs minerals are all at work again, providing the visitor with a real insight into the work which went on at Morwellham Quay.

The working museum is now becoming fashionable, so too is the interest in seeing history brought to life. Many thousands visit Morwellham Quay each year for a train ride into the mines and a glimpse of how life was when the quay prospered.

20

South Zeal
Doctor's Surgery in a Private House

WHEN Trevor and Joan Carr bought their house twelve years ago they also inherited a valuable community service: a branch surgery that had operated from their house for many years. Every Thursday morning Doctor Bell strolls up from his house and takes the branch surgery. It's handy for him because, at least one day a week, he doesn't need to journey to the Okehampton Health Centre and it's popular with villagers.

If it wasn't for this service local people would have to find the time and money to go into Okehampton. Mrs Carr sees it very much as a service to the village and one around which she fits her domestic life. The doctor has a consulting room, a waiting room and use of the bathroom. On winter mornings, as Joan Carr leaves for work, she stokes up the fire in her front room so that patients can wait in comfort.

Until two years ago the front room had another use on Wednesday mornings: the National Westminster Bank operated there from 10–11.30 a.m. Sadly NatWest decided to close down their South Zeal branch because of fears over security. Several other businesses had also closed in the village and it no longer made commercial sense for the bank to continue. For a time the Halifax Building Society picked up where the bank left off, but it too has now closed due to lack of business.

South Tawton Parish Council, who cover the village of South Zeal, undertook their own appraisal in 1981: this was a self-assessment of local needs, aspirations and opinions. One very practical benefit from this survey was that a voluntarily-run prescription collection service was started in response to local demand – patients are able to pick up medicines from the village post office. The family doctors also agreed to visit each person in the parish, aged seventy and over, at least once a year. A good example of community planning at its best.

21

Newton Poppleford's Surgery

GONE are the days of the village GP making stately progress through Devon's lanes in his pony and trap. In spite of modern communications, like the car 'phone or paging system, most villagers find that the only way to consult a doctor is to go into the nearest town. In Newton Poppleford, near Sidmouth, the story is rather different.

In 1982 the then Chairman of the Parish Council, Mr Compton, gave a piece of land to the village for a doctor's surgery. Previously, doctors from the two practices which serve the village used Mrs White's front room and the school room of the Methodist Hall. Graham Ward, a doctor from the Ottery St Mary Medical Centre

nearby, said there was something rather nice about consulting in someone's front room, but perhaps it was not quite in keeping with modern medical practice. Geoffrey Tenney, another former Parish Council Chairman, endorses the fact that it wasn't ideal and so with an available site being next to the car park, a public meeting was called to see how much support there was for constructing a purpose-built village surgery.

The project won enthusiastic local backing and was put out for tender. Original hopes of getting a building for around ten thousand pounds vanished and the final cost was nearer fifteen. The Parish Council applied a twopenny rate for a two-year period which resulted in raising £2,500 towards the required sum. The remainder came from donations and fund-raising events co-ordinated by the 'Friends of Newton Poppleford'.

Within eighteen months, after some forty-three events – which included a man in nearby Harpford rounding up stray cows and holding them 'hostage' until the owner paid a ransom of £15.00 to the surgery fund – the money was in the bank and building could begin.

On March 3rd, 1984, Mrs White, in whose house the doctor had held surgeries, cut the first spit to start the construction work. Now that it is finished there is a waiting room, consulting room and a small toilet. As Doctor Ward says, "It's a proper facility with security of tenure. Records can be stored there and you can do blood and urine tests with more confidence here than you can in someone's front room. The local people built it and are proud of it, so they look after it".

It's been used extensively since it opened in September, 1984 and Geoffrey Tenney explains its success: "I think that people are more at ease in the new surgery and if you don't have a car it's invaluable." Newton Poppleford led the way by providing one of the first community-built surgeries in Devon, at a relatively low cost. Perhaps more villages will follow suit.

22

Kilmington Village Halls

I T is debatable what constitutes the most important facility within a village. For some the church will top the list, others would give the pub their vote, but for many the facility that comes to mind most readily is the village hall.

In Kilmington, near the town of Axminster (famous for its carpets), there was great concern when the church room, which had been built in 1926 and served the village as a hall, ran into problems with both the fire officer and the Public Health Department. The Fire Service refused to renew the licence unless the wooden walls and ceiling were treated with fire retardent paint. The roof leaked, the toilets were unsatisfactory, and the boiler which drove the heating was on its last legs. The Parochial Church Council, the church's local governing body, couldn't possibly meet the cost of repairs to bring the building up to standard. After nearly eighty years (Kilmington's original hall or reading room was built in 1906 and now serves as the cricket and bowls pavilion) it looked as if the village might be without a hall – an essential meeting place for the community.

In March 1983 a public meeting was attended by about 130 adults from a population of 600. This is a measure of how concerned people

Kilmington's new village hall

were about the possible loss of their church room. The issue was simple – should a new hall be built in the village? The meeting concluded that about £8,000 was needed to bring the church room up to standard. The general feeling was that it would be better spent on a new hall – a village hall as distinct from a church one. Financial assistance is not available from the County and District Councils for a church hall, but it appeared possible to get a grant for a village hall.

A steering committee was set up (it's amazing how everything seems to start with the formation of a committee) to look into the feasibility of a new hall. The group of eight had to find a site before any detailed planning or costing could be done. A new vicarage was to be built in Kilmington, next to the church, and this was the starting point. In the planning application for the vicarage outline permission was also given for the construction of a new hall adjacent to the site. Who would own the site became the next matter for debate. Initially the proposal from the Church Council was that the site be leased to the village. Unfortunately, the rental looked prohibitive and so it was decided to raise funds and buy the site outright.

In July the steering committee reported back to another public meeting on progress to date. At this stage the projected cost was in the region of £65,000 but with architect's fees, planning fees and rising costs the final amount was £87,000. This was a massive sum and it was all hands to the pumps to raise the money. A target of this size might seem out of reach but local support was tremendous. Charity events of every description were organised and the money started to flow in. The first big boost to funds came from the sale of some land owned by the Parish Council. This swelled the coffers by £22,300 and the project was well under way.

It became clear that if the village could raise a third of the total, then grant aid to make up the difference might be available from East Devon District Council and the Community Council of Devon. Kilmington's seventeen different village organisations ranging from the Kilmington Players to the Mother and Toddler Group held events to help raise money. Donations also began to come in. In total the village raised £15,000, which together with the £22,300 from the land sale put the project on line for grant aid. But would the District and Community Council (the latter acting as agents for the Devon County) add their support as well?

Evidently the authorities were impressed by local commitment and following site visits, and some anxious waiting, the grants were approved. Only seventeen months since that first public meeting to discuss the apparently bleak future of their church hall Kilmington opened a new hall on October 5th, 1985.

The first impression of the new hall is of a modern, airy building which in style complements the vicarage next door. The front has a spacious car park and the hall overlooks the playing fields opposite, rolling farmland in one direction and the village in the other. The gardens and hall surrounds were planted and are now cared for by the members of the village Produce Association. Inside it is striking to find the stage positioned not at all where you would have expected – at the far end of the hall away from the main entrance – but to your right. Bert Cudmore, the Chairman, explained that this layout allows the use of the main body of the hall for badminton and keep fit without the stage imposing on activities. The kitchen and toilet facilities are logically near the main entrance and it allows good storage space either side of the stage itself.

The stairway inside the main doors, carpeted with Axminster donated by the local firm, leads to a committee room with glass panels that overlook the hall. The hall is an obvious source of pride to the village. To have raised the money and seen the new building constructed in such a short time is little short of a miracle. Everything seems to have worked out right, even the acoustics which can often be a hit and miss affair. The hall works equally well for drama and for classical recitals. It is in almost constant use by the various organisations who worked so hard to make this fine hall possible.

The Parish Council contributed another £5,000 to purchase the site and accepted trusteeship of the hall which is now a recognised charity. Financially, of course, having built the hall the story doesn't end there. The hall committee now have to cover running costs. They have continued to manage their affairs prudently and at the end of their first year the closing balance showed a profit of £3,000. The story of Kilmington hall is a truly remarkable one. It shows village spirit and co-operation at its best and where there's a will there is almost certainly a way. The accompanying photograph shows the old church room being demolished. As one chapter in the life of this enterprising East Devon village closed another began. Small wonder that the hard-working hall committee and the people of Kilmington are proud of what they have achieved.

Demolition of the Old Hall

Tavistock Community Bus

THE Tavistock Community Bus Scheme – one of five in Devon – started in 1981 to meet the needs of older people in Tavistock who found it difficult to use conventional bus services, either because there were none to their part of the town or because a steep hill separated them from the bus stop. This service also served a group of elderly people in Lamerton and isolated rural communities on the road to Chipshop. The community bus now provides a normal time-tabled service that is steadily growing. It charges fares in the usual way but differs from conventional buses in that the drivers are all volunteers as, in fact, is everyone else in the organisation. The routes have been extended so that the bus now serves a dozen isolated communities with a once-a-week shopping service; most of these places have no other bus service at all. Fares – and the occasional hiring of the vehicle to local organisations – cover day to day running costs, but the bus has to rely on government and local authority grants to cover major capital work.

The new bus can accommodate passengers in wheelchairs – and a regular 'Mobility Bus' service is also being considered. It is also clear that there is a demand for more than shopping trips and visits to the doctor – people have used the services for seeing friends and relatives or have just gone along for the ride, in some cases to see places they have not seen for years. The Community Bus Association feels that these are legitimate needs and is very happy to meet them.

Join the bus on market day in Tavistock – as it bumps down the long hill to Morwellham. Rounding the bend onto the cobbled quay, there is a small knot of regular passengers waiting. A cheerful greeting, a joke – and the passengers get on. A few boxes of plants come too, and eggs to sell to a friend in Tavistock. The driver collects fares and give tickets – 72p. return for the seven-mile journey. No one at the crossroads at the top – she doesn't come every week – so on through Gulworthy, to Wheal Josiah. The Council told us there were people there who needed a service and so we diverted the route to see if anyone would use it. A young couple with a small child get on – so the three-quarter-mile detour was worth it. Then down an unmade track leading to a caravan site and a row of cottages. 'Gran' to passengers and drivers alike is well over eighty but still travels into Tavistock when she feels able. While the driver turns the bus round in a space which looks hardly large enough to turn a pram, one of the passengers walks the last fifty yards down to the cottages to see if Gran is coming. She is, and a minute or two later she walks slowly up to the bus, climbs carefully on and proffers her open purse to the driver for him to take the fare.

Then it is on to Chipshop, Ottery and Mill Hill. The plants come off and more passengers, this time children, get on. The bus is now comfortably full. One more passenger waiting as we come into the town – then down into Bedford Square at the centre of Tavistock. Friday is a busy day and there are other country buses in the square – the Community Bus has its own stand and, for once, there is no car wrongly parked on it. The passengers get off – to go to the Post Office (for we have passed no Post Office on the way), to do a week's shopping and, if there is time, have a cup of tea. Presently the driver also goes for a much needed cup of tea.

An hour and a half later, having done three short trips within the town, the bus is back on its stand – and now it is left open so that the country passengers can board or put their shopping on before going to buy one or two extras. More passengers get on than came in earlier – some must have come into town by car – and there are a couple of people for a housing estate on the edge of Tavistock. All are welcome – although, by the time we are ready to leave, there are a couple standing and there are bags of shopping everywhere. The journey back is easier for the driver – there are fewer fares to collect. It is also slower because one of the passengers carries people's shopping in for them as we stop by their houses.

We leave the bus as it bumps down the long hill to Morwellham again, the day's work nearly over. It has been a busy day and the driver feels tired – but also content. The traditional market day bus is not quite an endangered species yet and the Tavistock Community Bus provides a service the old-fashioned way; it is a proper country bus and runs for the convenience of the passengers, not for that of some large company. The 'Community' bit – well, somebody backed his car into it the other day and the passengers were not too happy about what he had done to 'our bus'.

Brentor Community Shop

IN the space of three years Brentor, on the western edge of Dartmoor, lost all its shops and on top of that, the blizzards of 1978 meant that emergency supplies had to be brought in. At this point villagers like David and Gill Gorbutt decided to take some positive action: Brentor community shop was born on a sunny Wednesday morning in August 1978. Every Wednesday for seven years the shop opened from 10.00 a.m. until 12.30 p.m. in the church hall and was manned by a rota of volunteers. Other helpers collected goods and transported them back to base from a cash and carry in nearby Cornwall. The shop put on a 7.5 per cent mark up which covered the hire of the hall, shoppers' petrol expenses and incidental costs.

David Gorbutt comments that by 10.30 a.m. on a Wednesday, the church hall stage "began to look like a French café – which illustrates

the contribution that the shop made to the social fabric of the village''.

But times have changed and the nature of the village has altered considerably. About two years ago it was decided that the shop should cease trading. Gill Gorbutt says that ''with thirty volunteers on our rota serving a handful of people it became rather silly; the elderly and less well off have increasingly been replaced by younger more mobile families who have no problems in going further afield to Tavistock or Plymouth for their shopping''.

The influx of new families did give rise to a need for some sort of meeting point. The community shop has become a fortnightly mini-market, still in the church hall, where people can meet, have a coffee and buy home made cakes and preserves. Gill feels that the shop has become dormant but not dead: the mini-market serves a useful purpose in changed circumstances.

The community centre, run by a group of nine active and concerned villagers has introduced local film shows, a playgroup and community meals for special occasions. Last year they celebrated the end of winter and this proved a good way of bringing people together. There is also the flourishing *Brentor News* which keeps people in touch. David quips: ''We said that we'd take it on for four issues, but in the end, Gill completed ninety editions! It's well received and people get quite agitated if it's not out on time, which must be a measure of how much they enjoy it.''

The Gorbutts have recently moved to Tavistock, so the *Brentor News* has new local editors. The paper is going from strength to strength and has just celebrated its 100th birthday.

Brentor has a population of 374, many of whom are now transitory visitors who are conscious that they may soon be moving on. Gill observes that ''three-quarters of the houses changed hands once if not twice in the twelve years that we lived in the village.'' Brentor is a fascinating picture post-card village with three community halls and no real services. The post office was the latest casualty, closing after many years of service to the community: nobody was willing to take it on. A mobile grocer does, however, cater for the needs of older and less mobile members of the parish and a bus still links Brentor to the outside world.

As Brentor alters so the community centre has evolved new ways of meeting changed demands. All villages change for good or ill and it is impressive to see a place in which the community is willing to look after its own and adapt to new circumstances.

25

The *Scene* in Exminster

T ALKING to Gwen Bowles, editor and founder of *Scene in Exminster* you have an undeniable impression of warmth, efficiency, drive, and a love of her home town. It all started in 1978 when the Parish Council gave their blessing to the establishment of a genuine independent community newspaper. Gwen recalls that "the church magazine concentrated quite understandably on church news and although there was lots going on, there was a general lack of communication; really the top end of Exminster didn't know what was going on in the bottom end!" This is hardly surprising when you consider that Exminster has a population of over 1,500 and that there are current plans to build another 500 houses. Gwen has no doubts that "the village will double in size; we have become a dormitory for Exeter". This makes effective communication essential in a large, sprawling, place like Exminster.

Scene (as it is affectionately known) is delivered by thirty volunteers, to practically all households, by the first of each month. Their proud boast is "we've never been late in nine years!" The print run is 700 copies, with over 100 being sold in local shops. Volunteers either collect a £1.30 annual subscription or individual copies retail at 12p. There can't be many businesses that can claim, as *Scene* does, to have pegged prices for the last five years.

Scene in Exminster depends entirely upon volunteers: typists, collators, editor and distributors, drawn from a pool of about fifty people. Each issue is assembled by four different volunteers: "We try not to use them too often," Gwen continues. "I've always been a bit of an organiser – you can't expect to do a decent job unless you're properly organised".

Scene includes news, diary dates and features. 'Personality of the Month', focusing on a local character proved to be a particular success. *Scene* also carries a regular insert on behalf of the church, since the latter magazine became defunct. The cover features a local subject, which is changed every year, and each edition is coloured differently to tell them apart.

For ex-Exminster people there is no getting away from *Scene*. Twenty-five copies are posted to places all over England and some go as far afield as South Africa, the USA and Australia.

The only outside help for *Scene* came from the Community Council of Devon: grants helped to launch the first free issue and another went towards a typewriter. An old Exminstonian, a bookbinder by trade, is even binding the issues into yearly volumes for the local archives.

As *Scene in Exminster* toasts its first century, Gwen modestly says "it's a bit of a landmark," . . . and, without any fuss, prepares for the next issue.

26

Atherington: From Old Smithy to Village Shop and Hairdressing Salon

A FEW years ago the nettles in the back garden of Atherington's Old Smithy were waist high and you could see clear to the roof of the blacksmith's workshop. In 1986 the Old Smithy Stores and Salon brought a new service to the north Devon village. How did this change come about? The success story behind the shop is very much a family affair: Tony and Margaret Squire have lived in Atherington for many years; he is a builder and Margaret is the district nurse. Tony's practical skills came in very handy. With the help of his son David, an apprentice builder, they converted the redundant smithy into a two storey property. The village shop is run by Tony's sister, Christine Clemens, and upstairs the hairdresser is none other than their

daughter Alison! Christine's daughter also puts in time helping out with the shop. As Christine points out, "I left the comparatively leisurely life of a housewife and came into a full-time paid job; but with the support of the family you can manage both".

Early on it looked as though the shops might be refused planning permission: the county engineer thought that two shops would lead to an unacceptable increase in traffic. Fortunately, the county councillors – elected representatives who actually make the decisions – thought otherwise, and were led by their own Structure Plan to a final judgement; this states that 'Authorities can contribute primarily by considering sympathetically applications for permission to establish new shops, weighing community need against normal development consideration such as adequacy of access'. They decided in favour of the shops going ahead.

The Old Smithy Stores offers groceries, stationery, confectionery and fresh baked bread delivered from Chumleigh. Goods also come in from as far afield as Barnstaple and Newton Abbot.

The shop and salon lend each other practical and moral support: Christine and Alison compare notes, share their trials and tribulations and benefit from the company.

After two years as a businesswoman, Christine Clemens admits to being very pleased with how things are coming along. Given the support that the shop receives from the community, it obviously shares the sentiment.

27

Aylesbeare Post Office
Converted from a Private Garage

L YN STANSELL recalls "great consternation" in the village when it looked as if Aylesbeare would lose its post office. "Like everything else it's only when you start to lose something that you realise how valuable it is."

In 1978 the postmaster packed in the business after four years and sold off the post office as a private house. This left Aylesbeare to find a new postmaster and new premises. At the time Lyn was a busy housewife with two young children; as she stood one day at the back door chatting to a neighbour, they jokingly discussed the possibility of converting the family garage into a post office. That evening she tried out the idea on her husband, Martin. "He went white!" she recalls.

Meanwhile, the village was reaching new heights of agitation at the prospect of no post office. Lyn sent away for details and found that the Post Office were looking for someone to work from 9.00 a.m. to 5.30

p.m. five and a half days a week, sort out premises and security and receive only £1,100 a year for the privilege. A week or so later the Post Office came back and asked why she hadn't filled in the application form. With very little discussion they agreed to Lyn's suggestion of four mornings per week and that's how it's been since October 1978.

First of all they needed planning permission for a change of use: Lyn remembers the day when all eleven of the planning committee squeezed into the tiny garage cluttered with lawnmowers, garden tools and bikes. "They said how wonderful the plan was," Lyn recalls; "then they went away; we had our permission within three weeks!" The Post Office were equally helpful. Martin, a professional builder, created a room in half of their garage; a telephone, scales and other equipment were installed and the post office was open for business within two months of the original idea. Lyn now stocks 150 items but reckons that she still has "just a post office with a few extras." One of the postmistress's traditions is to open a flask of coffee at various times of day and share it with customers. There are no complaints and the post office is "very well supported", says Lyn.

The Stansell family are immediately welcoming and active within the community; as well as running the post office Lyn still finds time for W.I., country and clog dancing, swimming, riding and taking an evening class. Village services are fragile and depend upon the individual to succeed: under Lyn's effervescent management the post office has blossomed.

Lyn's attitude is crucial: "Please remember that you don't **have** to buy anything; just pop in for a natter and a read of the notice board if you like. That's what I think rural post offices are all about and long may it continue."

28

Kennerleigh Post Office and Stores

KENNERLEIGH is a tiny, pretty village about fifteen miles from both Exeter and Tiverton. Opposite a row of white, thatched cottages Edna Hammond runs the post office and village stores, and has done for the last twenty five years. It's been the post office and shop ever since she arrived in the village, and it remains a place where locals can buy a stamp, get their shopping or just pass the time of day.

There are only fifty-eight names on the electoral register and although Edna doesn't do giros or road fund licences she does provide a full range of other post office services, and more besides. ''I'm a message taker; if the postman can't deliver to someone in the village, because they're out, I take the parcel for collection later; the vet leaves stuff here for local farmers, that's all part of it.''

So Kennerleigh post office and shop is an important part of village

life? "I don't know. I suppose you ought to ask my customers how important. They do say the village finishes if the shop goes, so I suppose that it's fairly important."

Edna's customers must appreciate the service because some are still coming in quarter of a century after her arrival in Kennerleigh. "My customers are very faithful really, although new people moving into the village are not so inclined to support the shop but then they're not Devonians. In any case they don't stay, half of them. I don't think that country life is quite what they thought. It all looks very nice on a summer's day, but when they're snowed in, they don't think it's so good . . . I love it though."

That's when the shop comes into its own and the ever-present threat of large supermarkets fades a little. The shop has changed little since Edna arrived and it's easy to imagine that her cat has been asleep in the window, undisturbed, for some time. The post office too has remained much the same, although it used to be administered from Crediton, then from Exeter, and now the head office is partly in Exeter and partly in Torquay. When she's not busy behind the counter, Edna's spare time is spent in her garden. In the summer it's a blaze of colour and full of succulent looking vegetables, a testament to Edna's green fingers, and it provides her with a break from living on the job.

It's hard to imagine a place like Kennerleigh without the sort of service that Edna Hammond provides, but Edna is not getting any younger. With out-of-town shopping centres and the big Exeter and Tiverton stores not far away the future of small post offices and shops must be in doubt. It represents another aspect of life in Devon which is changing gradually but inexorably.

29

Blackdog Post Office, Shop and Garage

LESLIE BRADFORD and his wife Crystal run this amalgamation of three important facilities. Originally the Bradfords were the village wheelwrights, indeed Leslie is still officially Blackdog's wheelwright to this day although there's little call on his skills. The family then moved into the building trade, a business which Leslie's son and his son still run.

The Bradford family have run the post office in Blackdog since it opened, "getting on for a hundred years for certain," Leslie recalls. He can remember his uncle telling him how in the early days the post was brought in from Crediton on a pony, and later by horse and trap. "The trap used to go from Morchard Road to Rackenford; it would be out all day and then end up at Morchard Road station in the evening. It had a sort of box affair attached, in which they kept the mail."

Eventually, as on the farm, horse power gave way to the petrol

engine and motor cars arrived on the roads. "My old uncle had a petrol pump fixed. When he first started the petrol used to come in cans, along with the paraffin, by horse and cart from Tiverton. Mind you, there wasn't much call for petrol in them days as there was only two or three cars in the village."

Although the old petrol pump still exists, it doesn't work any more. Next to it the Bradfords have had a modern pump installed. As well as the garage and the post office, Leslie and his wife also run the village stores. "We just keep a few groceries and things like that, you know." It does seem, however, that if the Bradfords don't have it, then you don't need it; if you run out of anything out of hours you can go round the back, knock on the Bradford's kitchen window, and still get served!

The village used to have its own policeman. He's gone now, but not forgotten by Leslie. As a lad, Leslie swung on the policeman's gate and got his backside kicked for his pains. "Cor, he had massive feet. He only kicked me once but my God . . . I never hung on his gate again. No fear!"

That wasn't Leslie's only memory of 'the law' in Blackdog. One night while Leslie was at a party in the village, the family horse broke out. The policeman came along, caught it and penned it next to his own house. As Leslie was going home from the party, he passed the policeman's house. The horse neighed as it recognised him, so Leslie took it home. The policeman called round the next day and asked if he had seen his horse. " 'Yes,' I said, 'he's out in the field, quite comfortable.' Well, the policeman couldn't do naught about it but it wasn't very many days before he caught the old horse out again. He got in a bit of a paddy that time and summonsed us, and we had to go to court. The policeman gets up and reads from his book about finding the horse out in the road, when the solicitor jumps up and says 'You're the kind of chap that hides under hedges waiting for cattle and horses to jump out into the road!' Well, after that the case was dismissed. He was a boy, that policeman." Leslie chuckled at the memory.

Unhappily, Leslie's eyesight is failing and it can't be too long before he and Crystal decide to call it a day and put up the shutters for the last time. Whatever the future holds for them, when Mr and Mrs Bradford retire, it's doubtful if things in Blackdog will ever be quite the same again.

30

Trago Mills at Liverton

T HE story of Trago Mills really started when Mike Robertson left the army with a £600 gratuity and arrived in the West Country. He bought a restaurant in Cornwall called The Buccaneer. This led to his first brush with the planning authorities. Mike Robertson decided to change the restaurant's image by making certain improvements. Although these met with local approval they were frowned on by the planners who told him that he needed consent for the alterations. After a public enquiry, Robertson won the day.

Some time later whilst travelling the road near Liskeard, he saw a For Sale sign. The Ministry of Defence were selling the Trago Mills Ammunition and Gunpowder Factory, which dated back to the Napoleonic Wars. Mike bought the site, complete with tumble-down buildings, working water wheels and charcoal pits surrounded by woodland, and decided to sell off the remaining stock including old jerry cans and MOD scrap. This created such interest that Robertson next headed to Birmingham, where a timber merchant was selling up;

having successfully bought him out, he returned to Cornwall with a load of chipboard purchased at a knock down price, added ten per cent and sold it from Trago Mills within a few days!

Mike Robertson began to recruit staff but, being the man he is, this was done in a rather unconventional way. A man he picked up hitch-hiking in the early days of the business eventually became a director of the company. The firm expanded on the basis of buying up surplus or bankrupt stock and selling it on. The Cornish branch grew, again in spite of planning objections, and he felt that Devon should also benefit from a Trago Mills. In 1970 he bought the present site at Liverton near Newton Abbot. Almost immediately he ran foul of the planning authority and after going to appeal the Trago concept was launched in Devon.

The business at Liverton started from tin sheds and developed into an out-of-town shopping centre of 135,000 square feet selling anything from diamonds to dustbins. Although diamonds are no longer on offer, you can buy a £2,000 Chinese rug or a doormat at ninety-nine pence. There's employment for about 210 people at Devon's Trago Mills. At first they were self-employed but now everyone is a company employee. However, Robertson's clash with authority is not over. Trago Mills opens seven days a week which contravenes existing Sunday trading laws. Although the local council now recognises Trago as a major tourist attraction, Robertson is currently contesting his Sunday opening policy in the European Court – the test case centres on the Sabbath-day sale of a woman's bra!

Today Mike Robertson takes something of a back seat in the day-to-day running of the Trago empire, although he still writes all the advertising copy. More time is spent on designing a light training aircraft and masterminding extensions to Trago's attractions, such as a steam railway to take visitors through extensive parkland.

31

The Reopening of Yeoford Church

HOLY TRINITY CHURCH, in the small mid-Devon village of Yeoford, was first built in 1891. It's a small unimposing building which could easily be mistaken for the village hall or local school. Set back from the road, Holy Trinity with its squat bell turret sits in a small churchyard looking for all the world as if time has passed it by. The fact is that time almost did . . .

The number of people who attended services at Holy Trinity had been falling for some years and in 1974 the church closed. This is not a straight-forward process because the Church Commissioners have to start formal proceedings, issue a redundancy notice and move through a set legal routine before the church can be declared truly redundant. Spurred on by the finality of this procedure some of the village hall committee decided to look into the possibility of having Yeoford church reopened. One of those who became involved was Graham Brown who had arrived in nearby Crediton as a newly ordained curate. Yeoford lay within his parish.

One of the first tasks was to establish how much local interest there was in the possibility of Holy Trinity reopening. It seemed, following a village survey, that the interest was there but that several practical problems had to be overcome. While the church had been closed the electrical system had become dangerous and complete rewiring was necessary; the bell turret had begun to lean, broken windows needed repairing, some of the guttering required replacing and some new slates were needed on the roof, although on the whole the roof was sound and renovation work looked feasible.

Fund raising began and in due course the repair work started. The overgrown churchyard was cleared and once again Holy Trinity began to see the light of day. Using local labour the repairs were completed and in 1984, some ten years after closure, Holy Trinity once again opened its doors to a congregation. This was a candle-lit service, since the electrical work had not been completed. As the village grows through new housing so the congregation steadily increases in size. Now services are held every Sunday with a family service every second and fourth Sunday in the month.

As Graham Brown says, "The church here in Yeoford has come alive again and it's entirely due to the people of the village. It's brought the village together and the church is again a focal point in Yeoford. Had the move to reopen the church been based on sentimental reasons and nothing deeper than that, then the Vicar and I would not have supported reopening. It's all about a sense of commitment from local people and a feeling of need for this church to be open and now it's going from strength to strength."

32

The Rector of Sandford Parish

C HARLES EDWARDS does not conform to the conventional image of a country parson: he is partially sighted, albino and speaks with a strong American twang. He crossed the Atlantic in 1963 to become one of a diminishing breed – the parish priest.

Charles recalls his first country ministry in the village of Goosey, in Oxfordshire: "The poor Gooseyites had to put up with generations of young priests who were learning the ropes". Goosey was one of several places where ordinands were sent to preach as part of their ordination course at Ripon Hall Theological College.

Two demanding curacies followed in new or expanding towns that were being built while he was there. At Ware, in Hertfordshire, he gained valuable experience, running the parish church for nine months until the new vicar was installed.

As a team vicar in Basingstoke, he remembers, the growing

congregation spent most of its time "worshipping from a caravan while 1000 per cent growth went on around us!" The Church of England and Roman Catholic congregations joined forces to build a multi-purpose centre serving the surrounding estates. Charles admits that the move to St Swithun's, Sandford, "was the biggest contrast of my ministry". During his tenure church attendance has built up to around 150 (60 families); and no one goes unaccounted in the Rector's 'black book' – this lists all the houses, their occupants and telephone numbers and means that Charles can reach anybody in his care at any time.

He has a very flexible approach and treats everybody alike. "I don't make any distinction between church people and non-church. In that respect my classless American accent is a help – people can't automatically pigeonhole me."

In common with most country priests Charles covers a large, scattered rural parish which takes in several outlying hamlets as well as the main village. Sandford is part of the Crediton Group; team ministry in rural areas has been a rational response from the Church of England to declining numbers of ordained ministers and decreasing church attendance. The team approach works on the principle that several churches working together can be stronger than any one by itself.

Charles Edwards publishes the *Sandford Crossing*, a monthly digest of local news, views and diary dates. This is one very practical example of the church and community coming together.

At the end of our conversation Charles says that he must dash to sort out a school Eucharist, visit a woman whose husband is dying of cancer and pack off some visiting children for school – did any one say that the life of a country priest was easy?

33

Devon's Footpaths

T HERE are over 3,000 miles of footpaths and bridleways in Devon which form a network across the county. It's all very well having this maze of footpaths but unless they are used there is the ever present danger of them becoming overgrown, neglected, and lost for ever. With increasing interest in rights of way Devon County Council has sponsored a new post for a Parish Liaison Officer in their Engineering and Planning Department. It's a grand title for the job's present holder, Rosalind Mills. What exactly does it mean?

''As the County Council is the authority for highways, footpaths are their responsibility as well. Part of my task is to promote the proper use and awareness of rights of way in Devon. Over the last three years, the Manpower Services Commission have done a great deal of work enhancing and refurbishing rights of way, footpaths and bridleways, and the County Council wanted to make sure that people

Pupil from the West of England School for the Partially Sighted at a Lympstone kissing gate

knew that they existed and now that they have been cleared that these tracks are used. Since Parish Councils can take an active role in what happens locally to rights of way, my job is to help make them aware of what they can and can't do to maintain this county-wide network of paths.''

It all sounds very easy, as Rosalind describes it; just draw people's attention to their local rights of way and soon the footpaths will be crowded with ramblers, out for a stroll. But of course life isn't like that and so the 'Adopt a Footpath' scheme was launched. Based on an idea from South Yorkshire, it was refined and tailored for Devon and in 1986 Bishopsteignton became the first parish to adopt a footpath. The Parish Council enlisted the help of Devon's Probation Service and the community-service-by-offenders scheme, who undertake to keep the path clear and visit it three or more times a year as necessary. From there, Rosalind says ''it was very much like prodding or waking a sleeping giant, and sixty-four parishes have now adopted footpaths or bridleways. The interest is growing almost daily.''

Rosalind's job is very much one of public relations; a good relationship with those who live and work in the countryside is essential. There's little point in opening up disused bridleways and paths if resentment is caused. ''It's important to educate people to respect farmland and the wildlife they may meet walking these paths. We promote the countryside code and a close involvement between ourselves and the farmer or landowner. The last thing we want is confrontation. It's very very important that people work together. We can help farmers with the replacement of worn-out stiles and keeping paths clear – things that legally they might otherwise have to do. We can also help by clearly marking the route that a right of way takes and so avoid crop damage. If people don't know the route to take, then there's a danger that damage may occur so we can actually help the farmer in his work.''

The whole idea is very much a chicken and egg concept. If a footpath is overgrown then the incentive to use it vanishes. But there's an increased awareness now, not just because of the visitor, and at a local level there is renewed interest in maintaining assets that have existed for many centuries.

''The scheme has appealed to a wide range of people, from those who have lived in a place all their lives to the newcomer who has just moved into a village. People really do want to take an active role in looking after the countryside and preserving it for future generations.''

The County's policy of adopting a footpath makes good sense and will continue to spread across Devon.

34

Lustleigh Station

THE railway which linked Newton Abbot to Mortonhampstead had been closed for thirteen years when Mike Jacobs bought Lustleigh station in 1972. He came across the derelict site quite by accident. "I was looking for a property at the time and wrote to British Rail asking if they had any closed stations for sale; amongst the details of six that they sent, supposedly within commuting distance of Exeter, was Lustleigh. At the same time the Rural District Council had written formally to British Rail to complain about the state of the station which, they said, was spoiling the pretty village of Lustleigh."

The station and surrounding land cost just under £5,000. The question was how to set about converting Lustleigh Station into the lovely house that it is today. It had never been lived in and was a single storey stone building comprising a small booking office,

waiting room, a smaller ladies' waiting room (and even smaller toilet) a 'gents' and a lamp room. This came to a grand total of 550 square feet.

"Initially we turned the booking office and waiting room into a living room; the ladies' waiting room and loo became our kitchen, the gents' and the lamp room became a bathroom. We added an extension to the main station building which gave us two reasonably sized bedrooms. The planning authorities insisted, quite wisely, that the extension match the existing building as far as possible. It meant that the extension and the one we added at right angles at a later stage proved more expensive, because of modern building methods, but it was environmentally acceptable."

Outside the station, work is still in progress. "When you inherit about an acre of brambles it takes time to sort it out and the building was our first priority." There is a lawn at the back and front and the old platform acts as a patio and verandah to the house.

What's it like to live in an old railway station? Without hesitation Mike says "It's good. There are no ghosts and the only time I have heard the sound of steam or train whistles is when I put the appropriate records on! In fact my standard answer when people ask if there are any ghosts is 'it depends on how long you've been down at the pub'! When you do hear odd noises outside it invariably turns out to be a badger or hedgehog. It feels warm and comfortable and there's no sense of bad news about it at all."

Casual visits from the public are, happily, fewer than at first (although if people 'phone first they are always welcome) but Mike and his family regard the public's interest in their home with tolerance and some amusement. "I remember sitting down to Sunday lunch one time, when some people came along the platform past our dining room window – 'Oh look,' they said, 'it's a house and ther'e people inside it. . .' and that just about sums it up."

35

Feniton Station

FENITON STATION used to be Ottery Road and then Sidmouth Junction. Jack Cruwys can remember the station long before Feniton existed. He recalls the name of those who ran the signal box and the big monthly fat-cattle market with its accompanying horses and wagons, and pens for sheep and calves. He also remembers Miller and Lilley's coalyard with its own blacksmith's shop which attended to the needs of those horses used for shunting in the railway sidings. "In those days you could catch a train at eight and be in London by eleven in the morning – it was wonderful. I went up many times. It cost eight shillings return!"

This was the era of steam and Jack chuckled as he recalled the Whiteways cider train coming through on one occasion when the signal was set against it. "We was in the next field shearing sheep and we heard an awful noise, like a rumble of thunder. The train had to

stop on an incline, and some of the trucks became uncoupled and began to roll backwards and ripped up the track. There was cider all over the place and they had to run with a single line for a while.''

Another story of Old Sidmouth Junction comes from a local historian, Robin Stanes. He tells of the then vicar of nearby Payhembury who used to work on a leader for *The Times* newspaper in what was the Railway – now the Nogg – Inn. The editor's brief would arrive by locomotive from London, he would write the leader and put it back on the train in time for the next day's edition.

Alan Powell worked at Sidmouth Junction from 1956 to 1960. He was one of fifteen staff that manned the station. He remembers the Atlantic Coast Express (A.C.E.) stopping on its way through to Plymouth, Padstow and Ilfracombe; he used to detach coaches from the rear of the train to go to Sidmouth and Exmouth. Then Dr Beeching took a close look at the economics of keeping small branch lines like Sidmouth open. The death knell was sounded for Sidmouth Junction in 1966, although the Beeching axe didn't finally fall until March of the following year. At the end drummer Tony Marshall, on leave from the Coldstream Guards, sounded the last post, people wore black armbands and at Exmouth fireworks were let off. But these public displays of support came too late to save the station.

The last train to Sidmouth meant the end of an era. The signal box and sidings were shut in May and it looked as if Sidmouth Junction was going to fall derelict. However, Devon County Council had already agreed, before the station closed, that Feniton should be a 'key settlement' and the construction of new houses began. People coming to live in new Feniton now had no rail link into Exeter and were forced to use a Devon General Bus service via Honiton or Whimple. A pressure group, the Feniton Residents' Association, was formed to try to get the station reopened. After several years of campaigning British Rail did agree to reopen Feniton and today a single platform, which used to be brightened by Peter Hutchings' floral displays, serves the village once again.

36

Exeter Airport

E XETER AIRPORT, just off the main Exeter to Honiton road, is
owned by Devon County Council. Opened in the later 1930s, it is
now operated under contract by British Airports International and
provides employment for nearly 300 people in the administration,
maintenance and air traffic control sections.

Exeter serves the Channel Islands, with Jersey European based at
the airport. They carry about 60,000 passengers a year; charter
companies fly to Portugal, Greece, Yugoslavia, the Canary Islands,
Majorca and Spain catering for another 60,000 passengers annually.
Other scheduled services fly to Dublin, Belfast and Gatwick,
accounting for about another 30,000 in 1987.

Towards the end of the 1970s Devon County embarked on further
investment to allow greater use of the airport by package holiday
companies. The runway was extended so that bigger aircraft could

take off and land. The main facilities and navigational aids were improved to cope with the holiday traffic, which has steadily grown since 1980. Even Concorde has landed at Exeter!

During the same period scheduled air traffic declined but since Jersey European based themselves at Exeter airport traffic has steadily increased.

There are two runways. The main one is over 2,000 metres long and lit for use at night, with precision approach aids. The second runway is much shorter, with no lighting, and its use is confined to general aviation during daylight. Exeter is also used by the Post Office for internal mail flights to Liverpool and East Midlands airport.

The air traffic control unit at Exeter uses the Plessey Watchman, a medium range surveillance radar. This installation at Exeter was the first of its type at any civil airport in the country and although there were teething troubles, it now operates perfectly. This equipment gives air traffic controllers total control of the skies within a two mile radius of the airport.

The airport is also the base for Exeter Flying Club which accounts for the large number of small aircraft parked, taking off and landing at Exeter.

There's a tendency to dismiss regional airports as poor country cousins but a visit to Exeter confirms that all the services are on a par with city airports – a modern terminal building with duty free and other shops, bar, restaurant, customs and immigration. They all enhance an airport which links the South West with Europe and the Channel Islands.

37

Oakford – A Closed Primary School

OAKFORD PRIMARY SCHOOL was built around 1840 complete with two classrooms, fuel stoves, outside toilets and a coalshed. This Church of England School originally taught children up to the age of eleven. When middle schools were introduced the age limit was lowered to nine, which forced down the number of pupils to the extent that Devon County Council closed Oakford School in 1977. The building has until recently remained empty.

In 1985, the church settled legal difficulties and gained planning permission for the conversion of the school into a residence. A group of local people who wanted to reopen the school were outbid when the property sold on the market for around £20,000.

Children are now educated at Bampton First School which is about four miles away; the under fives used to be able to attend a playgroup and holiday play schemes run by parents in the village hall. The

brochure which sought to re-establish a school in Oakford states that "the sense of commitment felt by many of these parents makes them unwilling to accept the idea that this communal involvement in their children's development should cease when the children reach the age of five".

The prospectus went on: "The emphasis will be on co-operation between the children, their parents, other interested parties, and the teacher, to establish and provide for the needs of each individual child and to involve the school in the wider community and the community in the school." The idea was to set up a school along the lines of Satish Kumar's small school at Hartland in North Devon.

Although the Diocesan Education Authority was sympathetic, it needed to see that the local church community supported these proposals. Oakford Parochial Church Council were not in favour and so the school was sold as a private house, to the highest bidder.

Terry Mulvihill, one of the leading lights in the group which sought to reopen the school is quite clear that "many of the younger children and their parents have now left the village." Oakford had an opportunity to attract and retain young families – perhaps it missed its chance?

Plymtree
The School That Came Back From The Brink

SPRING 1982 brought nothing but gloom to the 300 villagers of Plymtree in East Devon's Culm Valley. A County Council report starkly announced that the school had twenty-four pupils on the roll with a staff consisting of the Head teacher plus one assistant. By the following September, it was anticipated, only sixteen pupils would remain. Consultations were to be held with staff, parents and governors, about the possibility of closure.

Declining numbers were blamed on the lack of community involvement and parents taking their children to schools outside the parish. But this small farming village was not about to stand by and watch its future wither. Alan Barnett, a parent and governor recalls that "The Plymtree School Action Group was formed at 9.00 p.m. on 21st June, 1982 – its birthday coincided with the birth of a royal prince which seemed a good omen!"

The first task was to survey all children under the age of eleven living in the catchment area. The results revealed enthusiastic support

for the school and blew apart the County's prediction that the school roll would continue to decline.

A profile of the school indicated that teaching standards were good, that children were happy, and that parents had ready access to the school. Journeys to alternative schools would have been long and difficult and the survey showed that the school roll was set to rise.

One hundred and fifteen people packed into the village hall to tell County representatives that they would be willing to put time, effort and money into keeping their school open. Their words were well received and the school was reprieved. Since then the community has been as good as its word. Many groups scramble at a time of crisis and then quietly fade away but the Action Group has evolved into the dynamic Friends of Plymtree School and have raised valuable sums of money for the school. There is good co-operation with neighbouring schools at Payhembury, Clyst Hydon and Kentisbeare. Children have shared in games, been on residential courses and jointly fielded teams in local sports competitions.

They have even had to sort out a new phenomenon – overcrowding! During the summer of 1986 a new classroom went up in the school grounds to cater for increased numbers. This was financed and erected by the Friends of the School with the help of the Royal Marines from nearby Lympstone Training Camp. Now more than fifty children attend the school.

Alan Barnett concludes: "The change that has occurred in the children of this village has to be seen to be believed: the Friends have provided the hard-working and enthusiastic staff with the extra assistance to make this possible."

Lawrence Tower

I F you scan the Haldon Hills, south west of Exeter, you can pick out the castellated form of Lawrence Tower. This triangular 'folly', also known as Haldon Belvedere, has withstood wind and weather since 1788. The castle celebrates the memory of Major General Stringer Lawrence, who returned from the Raj and succumbed to the English climate. The Tower was his epitaph from a loving friend. The word Belvedere derives from the Italian, meaning 'fine view' – an apt description of Lawrence Tower.

The story begins in the 1740s when Robert Palk, a native of Ipplepen (near Newton Abbot) went to India; the son of a wool trader, he rose to the position of Governor of Madras. *En route* he became friends with Stringer Lawrence, who was a founder of the British Empire on the sub-continent.

Sir Robert Palk, as he became, amassed power, influence and a personal fortune. This allowed him to buy up the Haldon estate which spanned several thousand acres of the Teign valley. Lawrence, who was a single man, spent much of his spare time with the Palk family on their Devon estate and became godfather to Robert Palk's son.

Stringer Lawrence died in 1775, at the age of 78. He is buried in Dunchideock church and has a monument erected by the East India Company in Westminister Abbey. Lawrence's portrait by the celebrated artist Sir Joshua Reynolds hung in the former India Office in London. Palk constructed the castle on Penn Hill (800 feet above sea level) where his friend, Lawrence, had enjoyed walking his pet spaniel. Such was the strength of friendship that the Palks continued to use the name Lawrence for their male line. The Belvedere was a place of entertainment which included a middle-storey ballroom complete with chandeliers. The castle was also an occasional summer house.

In the late eighteenth century Baron Haldon's dissolute son, Lawrence Hesketh Palk, acceded to the title. He gambled heavily and lost everything – including the estate. Lawrence Castle is now home to the Dale brothers, who open the property to the public (weather and circumstances permitting) every afternoon from 2.30 p.m. and in winter on Saturdays and Sundays. A spiral staircase leads to the top of the turret from which there are magnificent views of the Teign Valley. The panorama calls to mind Longfellow's verse:

> Thick with towns and hamlets studded, and
> with streams and vapours grey,
> like a shield embossed with silver,
> round and vast the landscape lay.

On a clear day you can see Exmoor to the north, westward across Dartmoor and north-east to the Blackdown Hills, while on the sharpest days even the Quantocks away in Somerset can be picked out.

Hatherleigh's Tar Barrels

REMEMBER, remember the fifth of November, Gunpowder Treason and Plot.

In 1870, the church magazine of the busy North Devon market town of Hatherleigh records – "our little town is very advanced in demonstrations and this year the Guy Fawkes doings were on a larger scale than ever. A tar barrel drawn through the streets at six o'clock in the morning and peals from the church bells disturbed and reminded us of the well known anniversary of the Popish Plot of 1605 (which in God's providence was frustrated). Then in the evening, at eight o'clock, a torch light procession (nearly 200 torches, the bearers dressed in various costumes), headed by the brass band, perambulated the streets. After the procession, the remainder of the tar barrels were drawn round the town, and the whole was concluded with a display of fireworks and a large bonfire on the Island."

The celebrations remain largely unchanged and on the Saturday nearest to November the fifth, Hatherleigh is still woken from its slumbers by this festival of fire, with an evening carnival to follow. Brian Doidge is currently the man in charge of the Hatherleigh tar barrels, although recent bad health has prevented him from actually taking part. "We buy or scrounge the barrels and then make up a sledge on which the three barrels sit. We buy a tar mixture from the local ironmongers and paint the barrels with several coats of this so that when they are first set alight the tar burns rather than the barrels. They are then dragged flaming through the town by the young men of Hatherleigh."

Over the years the route along which the barrels are hauled has changed. The Island mentioned in the Church magazine of 1870 became inaccessible in the early 1900s when the road was altered and until 1973/1974 the barrels and torches were burned in the town square. When the square was altered the pyrotechnics moved to the market, where the traditional event still takes place today.

It all sounds and looks highly dangerous but Brian Doidge is proud of the organisation and its safety record. "I've been doing it now for twenty years and there's never been any accidents that I know of. There's the odd cut finger or scraped knees where somebody has fallen over, but nothing serious. We only allow people over sixteen to pull the sledges and it's people who can look after themselves like the local tug of war team. Women can do it but we don't seem to have many women coming forward to volunteer."

Romantics may claim that the tradition has to do with gathering in the harvest and circling the town in fire to drive away evil spirits, but the connection between Guy Fawkes and the ceremony seems the most likely explanlation. Older residents certainly consider it to be a celebration based on Guy Fawkes' failure to ignite his barrels of gunpowder set below the Houses of Parliament.

Perhaps the origins of the Hatherleigh carnival have become shrouded in the mists of time, but what is certain is that on the Saturday nearest November the fifth the town is alive with excitement and the fire of Hatherleigh's blazing tar barrels. It is an experience not to be missed.

Computers at Yarcombe

WHEN Geoffrey Turner's wife gave up her job, four years ago, to start a family they had the idea of setting up a home based computer bureau offering word processing, payroll and accountancy services. The response was not good so they switched to supplying computer stationery. On his rounds Geoffrey realised that there was a market for redundant computers and so his company, Adwell, was born.

Computer technology changes fast and companies were only too keen to shift their stock and 'upgrade' to the next generation. This created a supply of second user equipment. Geoffrey found his market with firms that wanted to stay with and expand their existing

system. The first system that Geoffrey bought was a Commodore Pet – Commodore were selling stock returned to their factory under warranty and ex-display equipment. Adwell put in a successful bid and landed 120 units. Not only did the hardware come from Commodore but, on an informal basis, they put prospective buyers in touch with Adwell.

Some of the equipment needed repairing, so engineers and local staff were recruited. One of these was a local farmer with an interest in electronics. Extra space was required and this is where CoSIRA, (Now the Rural Development Commission Business Service) entered the picture. The Turners bought the Old Vicarage in Yarcombe which had an old stable block at the rear; with grant aid this was converted to provide an office, warehouse and workshop. Geoffrey found the planning authority sympathetic and the company now employs seven people – three engaged in selling, one full and one part-time secretary and two permanent engineers.

Interest in Adwell came not only from smaller companies but also from several industrial giants such as British Steel (BSC), the CEGB and even Cheltenham GCHQ. The contract with BSC led to exports to the French steel industry. The business has expanded very rapidly – turnover two years ago was £65,000 and now stands at £350,000, with Geoffrey predicting half a million next year – where does Adwell go from here? So far Adwell has concentrated on the business end of the market but Geoffrey Turner thinks that there is still an untapped domestic market for second user equipment. It's possible that with further expansion the firm might move from Yarcombe to a purpose built local industrial estate. Yarcombe has good communications with the nearby motorway and rail links. As far as Geoffrey is concerned ''Devon provides everything that I want for my family in terms of quality of life and working environment''.

42

The Supacat

WHAT'S the connection between the Devon village of Hemyock and Port Stanley in the Falkland Islands? The answer is simple: the *Supacat*.

Supacat is not as it might sound some kind of child's futurist toy but a motor vehicle of a very special kind. It's a six-wheel drive cross-country vehicle. It has low ground pressure tyres with both brake and skid steering. In simple terms this all adds up to a machine that can move over ground which other vehicles cannot manage.

The company which builds the Supacat consists of two men, Nick Jones and David Clayton, who designed and make the vehicle in a barn workshop just outside the village of Hemyock on the Devon-Somerset border. It's not cheap; each one costs over £15,000 and obviously is not a vehicle with general appeal. Although the firm has only been in business for seven years the two partners have already

produced and sold some twenty vehicles. So where have the Supacats gone? This is where the Falklands connection comes in.

The Supacat was used by the Royal Air Force prior to the construction of the new airport and runway at Port Stanley; nearer to home it is used in both farming and forestry work in Devon. The vehicle is produced to order and takes about two months to build. Seeing one put through its paces is a remarkable experience as is its ability to manoeuvre in very small spaces. It must have impressed the Ministry of Defence who purchased the Supacat for use in the South Atlantic.

Marketing is very important for the continued success of the vehicle; prospective buyers come from as far away as Ireland. Nick says of the company's record to date that "it's difficult to imagine how things could have gone much better".

Without doubt the Supacat is an impressive vehicle and a unique product from Devon.

43

Landowners at Sidbury

*C*AVE or *Beware* is the motto of the Cave family who live at Sidbury Manor, near Sidmouth, on the east coast of Devon. The private driveway to the splendid manor house sweeps through parkland where stock graze contentedly. To one side of a huge stone fireplace hangs the Cave family crest. Sir Charles' family were merchant bankers in Bristol and during the 1850s one of his forebears came to Sidmouth for a holiday. Like so many that have followed he ended up buying a house in the Georgian seaside resort.

He thought it would be a good area in which to buy land and create an agricultural estate. So the family sold quite a lot of land in north Somerset and Gloucestershire where they lived and had a small landed estate, and started buying up around Sidbury. By the 1920s they had amassed about five and a half thousand acres, a considerable estate. The plots were bought bit by bit, as holdings became vacant, and when an owner decided to sell he always knew that he would find a ready buyer in the Cave family.

One of the first purchases that Sir Charles' ancestor made was the title of Lord of the Manor and today Sir Charles remains the incumbent. Although in the 1980s the title carries no financial reward, Sir Charles still runs a manorial court leet, which was the forerunner of today's town or parish council. Each year on the third Wednesday in November the court meets at the manor house and the jury and the officials are sworn in. There are a reeve, a beadle, a pig and duck driver, a public crier and constables, none of whom have any power. Originally, they would have answered to the Lord of the Manor for the running of the estate and village. Sir Charles retains the records of the manorial court going back to the eighteenth century and intends to keep this tradition intact. He feels that as the years go by there's an increasing interest in such old customs.

During the 1920s Sir Charles' great grandfather died and some of the land was sold. When his father died in 1947 more land was sold which reduced the estate to its present size of two and a half thousand acres. Sir Charles' son, John Cave, owns fifteen hundred acres and farms four hunded acres on his own account. Sir Charles owns the remainder which includes the manor house built in the 1880s. On both parts of the divided estate there is a tenant dairy farmer; timber production and woodlands form a major part of their management.

Apart from its reduction in size the estate has also seen a greatly diminished workforce. The advent of mechanisation and changes in farming practice have brought a certain sense of sadness – times change and the old order passes away. Sir Charles himself is far from sad about it. A local magistrate and ex-High Sheriff of Devonshire, today's Lord of the Manor is not the forbidding figure that he might once have been. Sir Charles is keenly interested in the environment and the beautiful surroundings in which he lives; he takes obvious delight in his family and is determined that some of the traditions of the large estate owner should live on in Sidbury long after he has gone.

44

A Devon Councillor

G RAHAM ANDREWS is a large man in every sense of the word; the immediate impression is of a jolly, kindly soul full of robust energy. The latter is a quality that he must need because his work in local politics adds up to eighty or ninety hours *every* week. While the rest of us are wondering what to do with our increased leisure time Graham obviously has no problem in filling his.

Since 1967 he's been a member of Coombe Martin Parish Council in North Devon, where he lives. Through this he became a member, and then Chairman of the Devon Association of Parish Councils. He's also a North Devon District Councillor and, as if that isn't enough, he sits on Devon County Council as well.

How did Graham become so involved in public life?

"You start off with a certain curiosity about how people make decisions. Why, you wonder, did they decide to do that? It starts to grip you, a bit like a drug, and you want to find out what's going on behind those closed doors. Once you get in there though, you find out about all sorts of things that affect this decision making, things like laws. The layman, which I was at the time, just doesn't realise that. People have this concept of all-powerful people who get elected; a councillor in fact is actually somewhat restricted. I didn't understand that and a lot of people don't."

To illustrate the point Graham tells the story of a woman who came into his shop shortly after he had been elected to the Parish Council in May 1967. She said "Now you're a councillor, can you do something about the times of the trains at Taunton?" Graham chuckled at this memory. "Of course I couldn't but that's what I mean by people thinking that you are all powerful. A councillor can only do what the law demands or requires him or her to do, he can't do anything else. He's restrained by statute just the same as a Minister of the Crown".

Put like that it seemed perhaps a bit dull, and many public meetings can be deadly. So why does he work the hours he does? Can he really get any satisfaction from it?

"I just can't leave it alone. The 'phone will ring late at night or first thing in the morning and I can't not answer it. I have to know what it's about, what's going on. There's a lot of frustration about the job when you can't get your way and then it becomes very difficult, but there's a certain amount of satisfaction too when you achieve something: you see a development take place that you have helped to approve; or a road improvement for which you have been fighting for several years actually happens or you are really able to help some individual; then you think 'That's great, I did that!' Mind you, you don't often get a pat on the back for your pains. You get the complaints but only occasionally do you get thanks. The best pat on the back is when they open the ballot box and it looks as if they've voted for you once again."

45

Branscombe's Blacksmith

A S farming in Devon has changed so too have allied industries, trades and crafts. The laying of hedges used to be a job done by hand but today it has become the province of the tractor-mounted flail mower. Mechanisation has forced both man and horse from the land in search of a living. With the passing of horse-powered farming you might suppose that the village blacksmith would have disappeared, his skills no longer in demand. But the figure of the blacksmith abides and in the small East Devon coastal village of Branscombe she can still be seen at work. Yes, *she*, for at the tiny thatched forge owned by the National Trust, Lyn Bagwell works.

In these days of equal opportunity doesn't Lyn still find prejudice in what traditionally has been a man's world? Lyn is petite and it's hard to square her with the image of muscular arms pounding a horse shoe into shape, or the heat and sweat of the blacksmith's furnace and

the strength necessary to deal with a temperamental heavy horse. "It's a question of proving yourself," says Lyn; "if you can do the work and do it well, then people will employ you."

After a four-year apprenticeship Lyn doesn't work entirely with horses. Decorative wrought iron work makes up a large part of the working week, although horses remain her first love. The heavy French Ardennes breed is the biggest horse that she handles and diminutive Lyn shows no fear as she wrestles with a giant leg and hoof, lifting it into position on her apron where she pares off the old shoe ready for a new one. "You need a strong back for this job. Your back will make or break you as a blacksmith." Watching Lyn it's easy to see what she means, but don't these huge horses ever worry her? "Not really," she says with a grin; "it's just the evil ones which I get concerned about."

You need a good back, strength and it seems endless patience, all of which would be quite useless without basic skill. Watching Lyn at work and seeing what she produces from the forge, there's no doubt that she has all these qualities and more. Lyn's interest in horses extends beyond her blacksmith's forge, because she owns horses of her own. They are Morgans, an American breed that Lyn reckons to be one of the most versatile in the world. She has four horses and her ambition is to compete with them in the prestigious Horse of the Year Show in London. It may be that success in this field will further Lyn's expanding reputation as one of Devon's best blacksmiths. In spite of the rapid changes around her, Lyn Bagwell is helping to keep alive one of the country's oldest rural skills.

46

Woodtown's Gunsmith

IN Devon, someone who describes himself as a barrel maker might
well be producing beer or cider barrels, but Simon Mather works
not with wood but gun metal. He deals with the barrels of guns, and
although he can and does work on other parts of shotguns, like the
trigger mechanism and stock, it's the barrel which he is chiefly
concerned with.

Simon learnt his craft by serving a five-year apprenticeship in
London with Holland & Holland and then moved to a small London
gunsmiths' ''to gain more experience of the trade''. After a year he
moved to Devon and set up by himself.

In the workshop, set behind his small cottage in the North Devon
hamlet of Woodtown, Simon mainly works for three big firms. ''I
can't really survive on local work,'' he told me; ''there isn't that much
about.''

I thought that a gunsmith was a man who made and worked on guns. Not so, Simon explained: "Ther'e stockers who make the stock," (the wooden part of the gun which sits against your shoulder); "the engravers who engrave the metal surrounding the firing mechanism – and you can get really lovely engraving on custom made guns; I have known people bring in pictures of their own dog to have that engraved on their gun; then ther'e people like myself who work on the barrel; someone else leads it, and there's a specialist who makes the trigger and firing mechanisms."

Simon said modestly that engraving and the other skills were beyond him. "I wish I could do the engraving side of it, but you have to be artistic to do that and the leading, or blackening of the gun metal. I've got the chemicals to do it but I don't know the formula to get the right mix. That's a secret and only a few people in the country know it."

When his picture was taken Simon was in the process of adjusting the stock of a customer's gun so that it was more comfortable. This he did by putting the stock in a vice, wrapping rags round it and then pouring boiling linseed oil over it. Heating the wood and the application of sideways pressure from a piece of wood wedged against the wall carefully and gently persuades the wood to bend.

He was also pushing out small dents in the barrel, again with meticulous care. Aside from this repair work Simon can, of course, make a gun barrel from scratch. Having completed a new barrel it has then to be 'proofed', that is checked by the London or Birmingham proof house along with the gun's action, or means by which it's fired.

Shooting and guns are still part of rural life in Devon, although today it's much more likely to be clay pigeons than the real thing. Apart from any sporting interest in guns, a shotgun can be the farmer's last resort to protect his lambs against foxes or his cereal crops against birds.

Sadly, there's not much call for Simon to practise his skill making the complete barrel – "There are so many foreign guns about today people don't want English guns, although there's still a great demand for them abroad. My work comes mostly from repairs."

47

Dartington Crystal at Torrington

DOROTHY and Leonard Elmhirst set up the Dartington Hall Trust in 1925. The Trust originally concerned itself with many aspects of life in Devon and encompassed farming, industry, the arts and crafts. The Elmhirsts were determined to maintain the fabric of rural work and skills through support and encouragement, and also to develop and build new ones.

The work was centred in the south of the county at Dartington Hall. By 1966 the Trust was looking for ways to expand its work into other areas of Devon. Dartington Crystal was born out of this desire and has become probably the best know 'product' of the Dartington Trust.

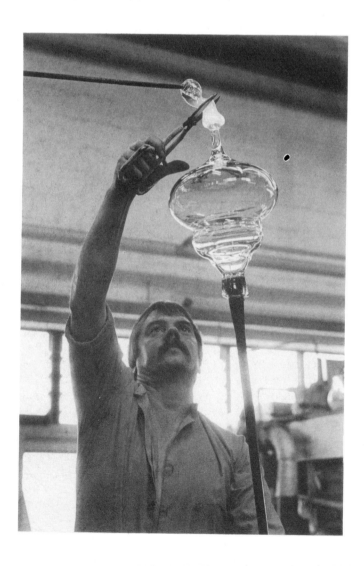

One of the Trust's aims has always been to improve the rural economy. Nevertheless the choice of Great Torrington in North Devon, an area hard hit by the decline of work on the land, was something of a gamble. The odds were heavily loaded against success. The venture depended on bringing to Devon people skilled in glass blowing, to start the enterprise and pass on their skills to local people who were recruited to the factory. Skilled workers came from Sweden, long experienced in glass work. The task of setting up the operation fell to Eskil Vilhemsson who arrived in Devon unable to speak a word of English. He must have found the dialect as difficult as the Devonians found his accent!

Vilhemsson set to work and some twenty years on, Dartington Crystal has built up a worldwide reputation. This is a measure of the sure foundation that he and the original thirteen Swedish glass blowers laid. When the factory opened in June 1967, they employed a total of thirty-six people. Today there are over 250 employees. Dartington Crystal is unique in several ways: it is the only English Company that produces uncut crystal glass-ware and early on they saw the potential of opening the factory to visitors, so that people can see the glass actually being made.

Most of the designs are by Frank Thrower and the end result is a hand-made product of remarkable quality. A measure of its design excellence and execution is that, when in 1986 an exhibition of the hundred best-ever designs was mounted at London's Victoria and Albert Museum, there was a Dartington Champagne glass alongside Concorde and the Morris Minor car! Both Eskil Vilhemsson and Frank Thrower have been recognised for their contributions to the glass industry; Eskil was awarded the OBE and Frank the MBE in 1987.

To visit Dartington is to marvel at the skill and speed of the craftsmen. Glass blowers work in varying sized teams, depending on the item being produced, and use raw glass manufactured from a secret Dartington formula – they would not divulge the recipe! The molten glass is taken from furnaces where it has been heated overnight to temperatures of 1,400 degrees centigrade and the first bubble is blown. The item is blown into a mould and the base or stem added afterwards. It is then slowly cooled, the waste trimmed off, washed and checked for quality and then packed ready for sale to places as far away as the Falklands and America.

It's small wonder that the making of Dartington crystal brings 150,000 visitors a year to the factory. It is fascinating to watch the highly skilled workers producing the glassware by traditional means. There is also an exhibition of glass through the ages and a replica glass cone, at which workers in costume demonstrate how glass was made two hundred years ago.

Dartington Crystal has come a long way since its birth twenty years ago. The Trust's gamble has more than paid off, with Dartington's reputation taking a Devon product to the rest of the world.

48

The Sisters of Posbury

T HE Franciscan Order of The Servants of Jesus and Mary came to the tiny hamlet of Posbury, near Crediton, in 1942 from the Isle of Wight. The sisters settled in Devon when the government of the day made it clear that if an invasion came, the small island off the south coast would not be defended. All 'non-essential personnel' were, therefore, evacuated to the mainland.

The sisters found their home deep in rural Devon, where in summer the hedgerows almost strangle the lanes which run between them, bisecting the fields and hills which have remained unchanged for centuries. During the war large rambling houses were unwanted so the Order picked theirs up for song. The sight of the sisters in brown serge habits with their unusual head-dresses became part of country life in this part of Devon.

Today, the Order or Community has only six members. Any notion

of a strict routine or closed order would be quite wrong. The sisters have many visitors – over two thousand a year – who come to stay on retreats; these provide an opportunity to step outside the hurly-burly of modern life and recharge the spiritual batteries. The sisters also travel far afield to tell people about their life at Posbury.

The day starts at 6.15 a.m. First Office is held in the tiny chapel, converted from the old stables. This is followed by Holy Communion, breakfast, another Office in the chapel and then work on the farm, in the house or kitchen. There is an hour for lunch and relaxation before the afternoon work which finishes at about 4.30. After high tea, vespers is succeeded by recreation and the last two Offices of the day before bed.

The sisters live on a total of thirty-six acres, ten of which are woodland. They grow one and a half acres of vegetables and just under an acre of pears, apples and plums. Previously, the land was worked by hand but today they have two rotavators and a small tractor; Sister Mary, who trained at horticultural college, keeps up with modern farming methods and finds the neighbouring farmers very kind and helpful.

The produce sustains the sisters and their visitors – "peas picked that

morning taste very different to what you buy in the shop" – and much of their time is spent on the farm and gardens. They don't have television, video or a dishwasher. They do have a wireless, mainly for getting the right time, a washing machine and take a daily paper to keep in touch with what's going on in the outside world. In no sense are they isolated, and indeed have to earn their living as anyone else. The retreats generate some income, paying guests and the sale of plants and small gifts bring in more money, while the produce is self financing.

Is their life one of sacrifice? "It might be to begin with, but my word you get the hundred fold in daily living. It's fulfilment that your're doing what God asks you to." What does the future hold for the sisters of Posbury? Sister Mary sums it up very simply: "I don't know at all. The Lord hasn't made it clear to us that he wants us to change and do something else and until he does there's no point in making plans."

For the time being the sisters will continue as they have for decades, and for centuries before their move to Devon: life for them has changed little. The modern world has not passed them by, rather they have chosen not to allow too much of it to encroach into their world. The sisters don't resist change or development, it's just that some of it is not allowed to affect them. In many ways their attitude epitomises 'Changing Devon': changes come, more will follow, and some are to be welcomed while others should be rejected. Perhaps it is only from their tranquil, obviously happy and peaceful standpoint that any objective decision can be made as to which is which.